Questions Concerning Health

Stress and Wellness in Johannesburg

T0327308

SOUTH AFRICA

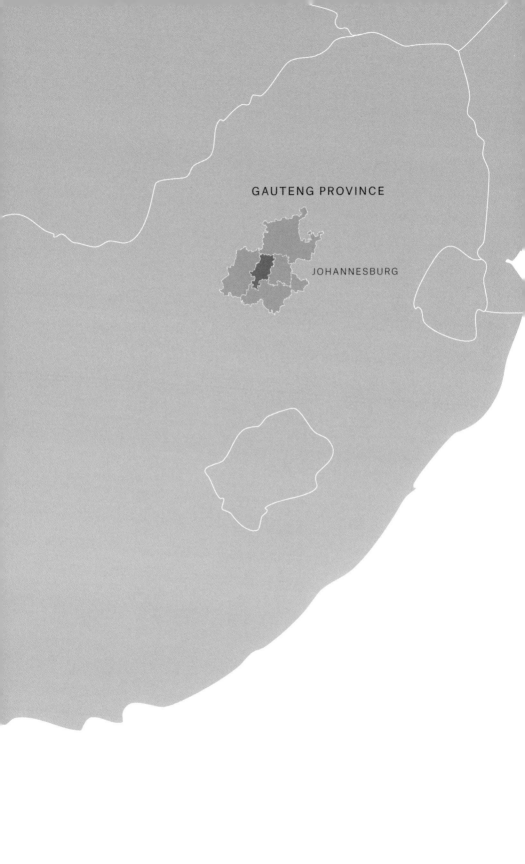

GAUTENG PROVINCE

JOHANNESBURG

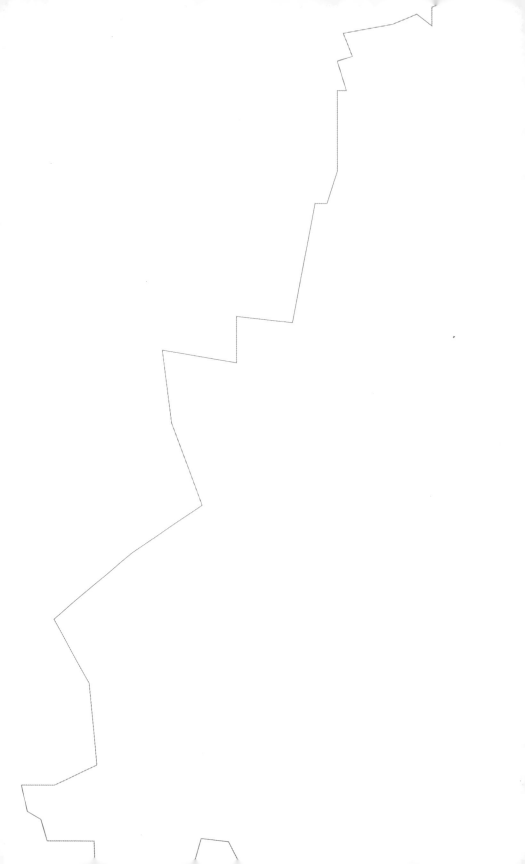

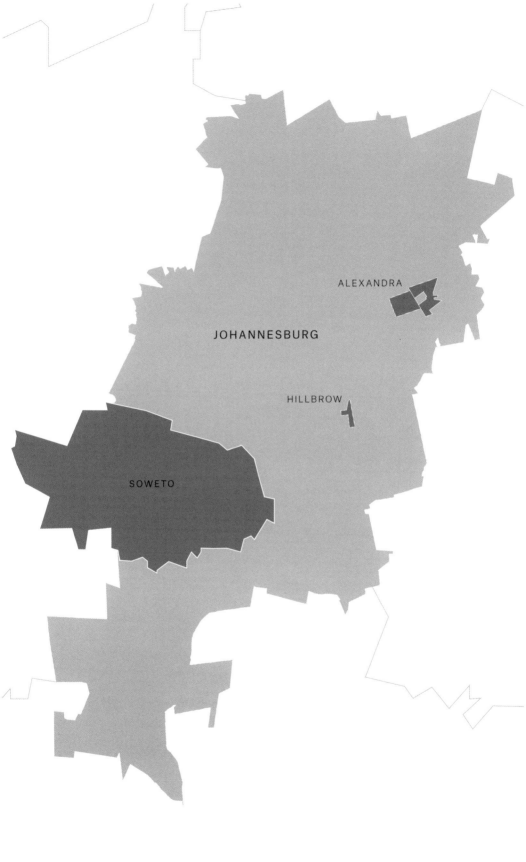

VIEW OF HILLBROW LOOKING NORTH FROM THE ROOF OF THE MARISTON HOTEL
GUY TILLIM, JO'BURG, 2004

Questions Concerning Health

Stress and Wellness in Johannesburg

Edited by Hilary Sample

GSAPP BOOKS

Columbia University
Graduate School of Architecture, Planning and Preservation

Essays

Case Studies

Maps and Research by Allison Schwartz

Symposium

Walking Maps

Proposals

Foreword

Amale Andraos

Amale Andraos is Dean of Columbia University's Graduate School of
Architecture, Planning and Preservation

In *Questions Concerning Health: Stress and Wellness in Johannesburg*,
Professor Hilary Sample brings us into territory she is pioneering—the
overlapping terrain of architecture, cities, and public health. Urban public
health emerges for Professor Sample as a sharp tool to cut through the
past decades of architectural discourse: Engagement, yes, but how?
Moving beyond the notion of the "architect-at-large," Professor Sample's
research invites us to consider new forms of architectural practice that,
while deeply embedded within the discipline, open toward fields like
public health, finding newly framed and increasingly charged modes of
engagement with the city. How can two disciplines, architecture and
public health, both formed by and forming the built environment, have
existed separately for so long? How can this separation continue when
their mutual influence is so critical to our understanding and designing of
the future of architecture and of cities? These are the questions Professor
Sample asks.

Questions Concerning Health situates the work of the advanced design
studio Stress and Wellness, which Professor Sample led in the spring of
2014 at Columbia University's Graduate School of Architecture, Planning
and Preservation, within a larger context of essays, case studies, and
debate around the question of urban public health. Building on Sample's
own research as well as on her growing network of colleagues and expert
collaborators, it stands as testimony to her success in fostering this new
conversation. As a body of thinking, design research, and register of
methodologies, the book is a wayfinder for those sites at which architecture and public health intersect. And in a simple yet powerful way, the
work demonstrates the possibilities that emerge from such interdisciplin-
ary thought.

Questions Concerning Health offers architects and students of architecture a fresh and provocative way to analyze cities today, one that builds on the recent history of architects' experimentation with urban mappings—from Venturi Scott Brown's seminal *Learning from Las Vegas* to Rem Koolhaas' *Harvard Project on the City* series—by proposing urban public health as a way to recast the relationship between architecture and cities. In doing so, *Questions Concerning Health* ushers in a new tone for this type of engagement. No longer satisfied with simply documenting the effects of globalization and rapid urbanization, it asks architecture to rise to the urgent health challenges facing cities and people of the world and of developing countries in particular.

This newly triangulated relationship among architecture, cities, and public health moves the conversation, as Professor Sample suggests, beyond *S,M,L,XL* to demonstrate the importance of reclaiming the small. When even the smallest of buildings can have the greatest influence on the global landscape of urban health and disease, the relationship between the small and the extra–large can no longer be understood as linear, with an increase in size pointing to greater complexity, impact, and importance, but rather as always nested with the possibility for the relationship between size and status to be at times proportionately inverted.

This heightened care for the nested scales of the street and the neighborhood, embraced as worthwhile frames through which to grasp the complexity of the larger forces shaping cities, is reminiscent of Team X and the Smithsons' habitat: "The principles of a community's development can be derived from the ecology of the situation, from a study of the human, the natural, and the constructed, and their action on each other," writes Alison Smithson, reflecting on the "Doorn Manifesto." Yet the essays herein speak with an added sophistication, resisting the casting of this specific South African city as either romantic or exotic, as the forays of 1960s architects in North African cities at times did. As such, *Questions Concerning Health* carefully adds to the body of knowledge that constitutes the context for learning and practicing architecture today, expanding the canon from within rather than positing the context of Johannesburg as an "other" by which to reassert the core. As an outcome

Andraos

of the Columbia GSAPP's Studio-X project—a pioneering, unconditional, and urgent commitment to the final eradication of center-periphery narratives in architecture schools—*Questions Concerning Health* sets a model and standard for how new knowledge can be produced through design research and speculation.

The question of public health recasts the relationship between the local and the global in important other ways as well. As the collection of essays in the book suggests, it establishes a common ground for a new conversation among various experts and reasserts the critical importance of collaborative work in today's practice of architecture, as we think through the challenges facing our cities and imagine alternate models for the future. More importantly, the lens of urban public health, as embodied in the research and case studies as well as in the studio's speculative projects contained in this book, offers a strong and inspiring way to reassert the local and its specificity beyond reductive expressions of identity, cultural difference, or the constructed opposition between tradition and modernity that continues to spread through the landscape of global architecture today.

23.2%
of population is aged 0–14

72.7%
is of working age (15–64)

4.1%
of population is over 65

25%
unemployment rate

81.4%
live in dwellings

64.7%
have piped water inside dwelling

90.8%
have electricity

DATA: SOUTH AFRICA, STATISTICS SOUTH AFRICA 2011

1990 63 years

2000 57 years

2011 58 years

Life expectancy at birth, both sexes

DATA: SOUTH AFRICA, WORLD HEALTH ORGANIZATION

Preface

Hilary Sample

Hilary Sample is an Associate Professor of architecture at Columbia University, Graduate School of Architecture, Planning and Preservation. She is also a principal of MOS Architects.

For an architect, practice today can absorb an array of influence, but there is perhaps no greater influence than the city as a source of creating architecture and thinking about design. Within this thinking, it is time to refine our approach to design and to reinvent how architects not only look at the world at large but also how we engage the world and, subsequently, how we practice. The development of the city has always included both the subjects of architecture and health, two seemingly disparate disciplines. Specifically, urban public health is not considered an allied field to architecture in the way that art or engineering is. Yet, urban public health is undoubtedly a measure of the built environment. Increasingly, the world, cities, neighborhoods, and buildings are affecting one another with greater speed and across scales. We are no longer a world of *S,M,L,XL*, but are learning how local health is critical to urban health and how the local, or even the building scale, can influence or be influenced by the global. While architects learn how to operate in and between these scales, one area that must be examined is the local condition on the personal scale — neighborhoods, public spaces and routes of circulation.

What this mode of inquiry requires is a more inclusive definition of architecture. If architects have long since expanded their team of experts to include structural and civil engineers, the future will require including public health experts. This goes beyond working with doctors on hospitals and clinics to draw upon a knowledge of health in general architectural practice. Public health experts and epidemiologists spend more time in the city than architects, urban designers, or planners do. They work collaboratively, they produce maps, and their work results in public policy. Architects can and should do more of this through design. Architects and public health experts could have a greater relationship to one anothers' work if only they were able to better communicate final

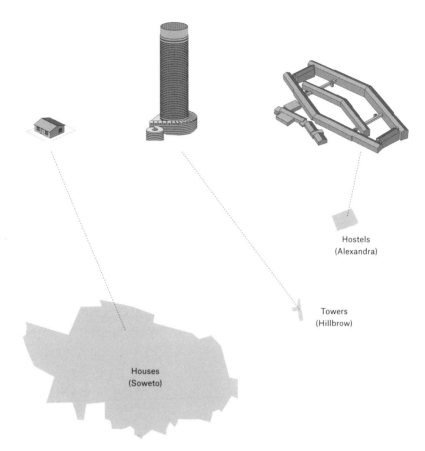

SPATIALITY OF DIFFERENT HOUSING TYPOLOGIES IN JOHANNESBURG

Hostels
(Alexandra)

Towers
(Hillbrow)

Houses
(Soweto)

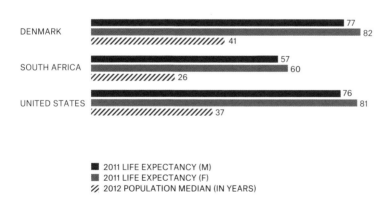

DENMARK — 77 — 82 — 41

SOUTH AFRICA — 57 — 60 — 26

UNITED STATES — 76 — 81 — 37

■ 2011 LIFE EXPECTANCY (M)
■ 2011 LIFE EXPECTANCY (F)
/// 2012 POPULATION MEDIAN (IN YEARS)

LIFE EXPECTANCY AND MEDIAN AGE
DATA SOURCE: WORLD HEALTH ORGANIZATION STATISTICS SUMMARY

projects or representations, or public exhibitions of their work. We need to work in parallel—this is without question—but where and when we connect needs to be understood sooner rather than later. It is my hope that this report creates such a connection.

In spring 2014, eight students from Columbia University's Graduate School of Architecture, Planning and Preservation (GSAPP) traveled to Johannesburg, South Africa, to better understand the implications of stress and wellness at the intersection of urban public health, architecture, and cities. In a time of increasing urbanization, Johannesburg is a setting unlike any other. The city has had an embattled history, from the social crisis of apartheid to the health crisis of HIV/AIDS. Its urban development bears traces of this history, from squatter settlements in the Hillbrow neighborhood to dormitories in Alexandra and government housing in Soweto. For this reason, it served as the focus of the studio as a stressed urban environment that warrants further architectural study.

Prior to the trip, students and faculty struggled to gain access to complete health data, whether in the form of maps or statistics. Access to information on health in Johannesburg is limited, with many key documents found only in archives and libraries. Therefore, students learned about the city in part by studying urban patterns through Google Maps, reading selected texts, and referencing international and national demographic and health data.

Throughout the term, the studio questioned assumed notions of global health, instead asserting that health is local. This key concept would later be expanded upon by lectures and symposia aligned to key developments within the studio. Driving, and at times confounding, the students' work was a need to study the city at close range and to intensify the relationship between site and studio, city and architecture—in spite of the great physical distance between New York and Johannesburg. Undertaking critical research before traveling prepared the students for the field work of observing and documenting neighborhoods, experiencing a variety of urban spatial typologies—from taxi ranks to hospitals and housing towers—and exposed the students to urban stress first-hand by studying how

Sample

the city has evolved since the end of apartheid. Uncovering recent history with respect to urban form led the students to focus on three particular areas: Hillbrow in Central Johannesburg, the Bara area within Soweto, and Alexandra.

The epidemiological term "social equivalency" became an important concept for the studio. In social distancing, two places that share symptoms of the same disease are considered to be close even if their physical proximity is geographically distant. Social distancing is perhaps greatest in Johannesburg when measured against places like New York or Copenhagen, which the students visited and studied as part of the term, to compare housing models and climate. Johannesburg's public health crises, from the legacy of apartheid, the AIDS/HIV pandemic, and poverty, to its stressed urban infrastructures, decayed buildings, and increasing immigrant population, makes the city an exemplary place for studying the relationship between the city and health.

What we learned is that today, health is above all local, and this condition requires intensively local architectural responses. The studio learned about the multifaceted problems of urban stress and found moments of optimism through a variety of responses concerned with wellness, including new housing types, new forms of workspaces, building repair guilds, shelters for victims of gender-based violence, and a new energy center. Johannesburg is a city that is continually changing and rapidly shifting. Its fluctuations further the idea that health is significantly local. In response to that, architects and designers face greater challenges but also opportunities for rethinking the relationship of form to its environments.

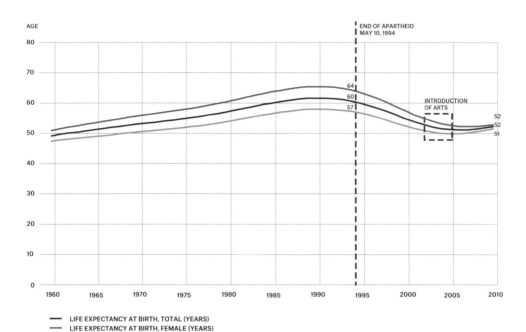

LIFE EXPECTANCY, SOUTH AFRICA
DATA SOURCE: WORLD BANK, WORLD DATABANK, 2013

TOTAL POPULATION   5,598,000   318,000,000   52,386,000

DENMARK	UNITED STATES	SOUTH AFRICA

PERCENTAGE OF POPULATION LIVING IN URBAN AREAS

87%	82%	62%

URBAN POPULATION
DATA SOURCE: WORLD HEALTH ORGANIZATION STATISTICS SUMMARY, 2012

Sample

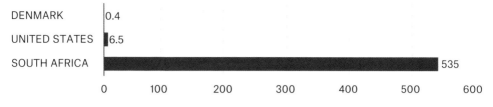

DEATHS DUE TO HIV/AIDS (PER 100,000 POPULATION)
DATA SOURCE: WORLD HEALTH ORGANIZATION STATISTICS SUMMARY, 2011.

PREVALENCE OF HIV AMOUNG ADULTS AGED 15 TO 49 (%)
DATA SOURCE: WORLD HEALTH ORGANIZATION STATISTICS SUMMARY

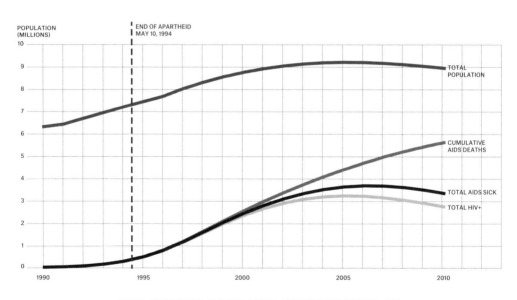

TOTAL POPULATION, NUMBER OF HIV+ AND AIDS SICK PEOPLE AND
CUMULATIVE AIDS DEATHS, GAUTENG PROVINCE
DATA: D. BRADSHAW, D. BUDLENDER, AND R.E. DORRINGTON, HIV/AIDS
PROFILE OF THE PROVINCES OF SOUTH AFRICA—INDICATORS FOR 2002,
CENTRE FOR ACTUARIAL RESEARCH, MEDICAL RESEARCH COUNCIL
AND THE ACTUARIAL SOCIETY OF SOUTH AFRICA, 2002

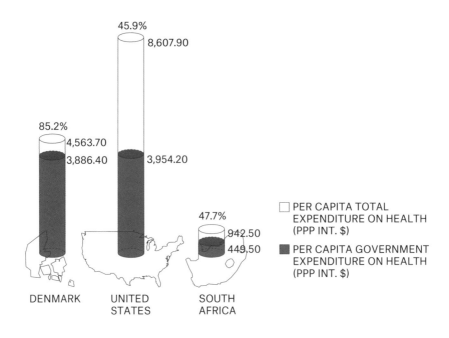

45.9%
8,607.90

85.2%
4,563.70
3,886.40   3,954.20

47.7%
942.50
449.50

☐ PER CAPITA TOTAL
EXPENDITURE ON HEALTH
(PPP INT. $)

■ PER CAPITA GOVERNMENT
EXPENDITURE ON HEALTH
(PPP INT. $)

DENMARK   UNITED   SOUTH
STATES   AFRICA

EXPENDITURE ON HEALTH CARE
DATA SOURCE: WORLD HEALTH ORGANIZATION
STATISTICS SUMMARY, 2011

DENMARK   16.4%
SOUTH AFRICA   12.7%
UNITED STATES   19.8%

GOVERNMENT EXPENDITURE ON HEALTH
DATA SOURCE: WORLD HEALTH ORGANIZATION
STATISTICS SUMMARY, 2011

DENMARK   10.8
SOUTH AFRICA   81.1
UNITED STATES   59.3

PRIVATE PREPAID PLANS AS A PERCENTAGE OF PRIVATE
EXPENDITURE ON HEALTH DATA SOURCE: WORLD HEALTH ORGANIZATION
STATISTICS SUMMARY, 2011

26

Sample

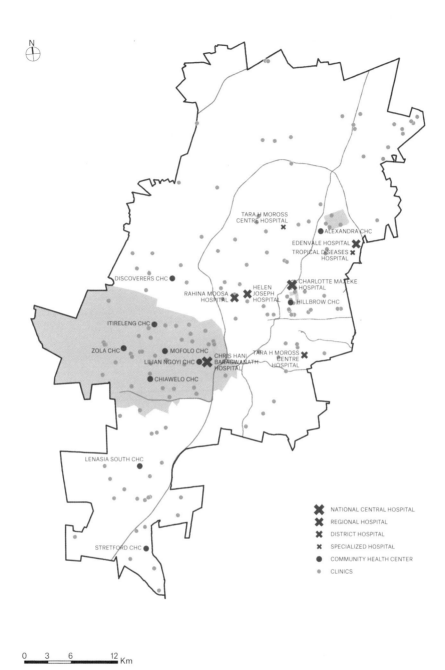

N

TARA H MOROSS
CENTRE HOSPITAL ✖
● ALEXANDRA CHC

EDENVALE HOSPITAL ✖
TROPICAL DISEASES ✖
HOSPITAL

DISCOVERERS CHC ●

CHARLOTTE MAXEKE
✖ HOSPITAL

RAHINA MOOSA   HELEN
HOSPITAL   ✖ JOSEPH
HOSPITAL   ● HILLBROW CHC

ITIRELENG CHC ●

ZOLA CHC ●   ● MOFOLO CHC

LILIAN NGOYI CHC ✖   TARA H MOROSS
CHRIS HANI ✖   CENTRE
BARAGWANATH   HOSPITAL
HOSPITAL

● CHIAWELO CHC

LENASIA SOUTH CHC ●

STRETFORD CHC ●

✖	NATIONAL CENTRAL HOSPITAL
✖	REGIONAL HOSPITAL
✖	DISTRICT HOSPITAL
✖	SPECIALIZED HOSPITAL
●	COMMUNITY HEALTH CENTER
●	CLINICS

0   3   6   12 Km

CITY OF JOHANNESBURG PUBLIC HEALTH FACILITIES
SOURCE OF HEALTH FACILITIES: DISTRICT HEALTH INFORMATION
SYSTEM (DHIS), GAUTENG PROVINCE, 2013

Introduction

Mpho Matsipa

Mpho Matsipa is a lecturer in the Wits School of Architecture and Planning at the University of Witwatersrand in Johannesburg, and is working toward her Ph.D. in architecture and African urbanism at the University of California, Berkeley. She is director of Studio-X Johannesburg.

When Salman Rushdie wrote the following words, he was describing Los Angeles:

> In such a city there could be no grey areas, or so it seemed. Things were what they were and nothing else, unambiguous, lacking subtleties of drizzle, shade and chill. Under scrutiny of such sun there was no place to hide. ... No mysteries here or depths; only surfaces and revelations. Yet to learn the city was to discover that this banal clarity was an illusion. The city was all treachery, all deception, a quick-change, quicksand metropolis, hiding its nature, guarded and secret in spite of all its apparent nakedness.[1]

Rushdie could just as easily have been describing São Paulo, but also Johannesburg—a booming metropolis, and the financial center of South Africa.

Johannesburg bears the traces of a profoundly segregated and contested national and urban history. And yet, as noted by Martin Murray, contemporary Johannesburg also shows signs of a more contemporary "splintering urbanism," a poly-nuclear urban form of divisive networked infrastructure, shopping malls, and gated communities that bypass the poorer, peripheral parts of the city—which are nevertheless essential to its own survival. One might even argue that a colonial city like Johannesburg, with its unequal and fragmented urban form, prefigures the splintering urbanism that Steven Graham and Simon Marvin outline so brilliantly in their 2001 book by the same title.

The greater Johannesburg metropolis covers an area of 2,300 square kilometers, making it larger than Sydney, London, or New York, and similar in size to Los Angeles.[2] The whole urban conurbation, comprised of Johannesburg, Pretoria, and the East Rand metropolitan area, is estimated at between six and seven million people. With the country's population at approximately fifty million, this combined metropolitan region accounts for 17 percent of all South Africans.

Johannesburg's inner city is a "contact zone" for many business activities and urban residents. The inner city is the focus of the primary transport interchanges in Johannesburg. Eight hundred thousand commuters enter the CBD every working day in Johannesburg. Approximately 200,000 people work there daily, and it is also a major destination for traders and shoppers from across the subcontinent, as well as being home to a number of head offices of many premier legal and financial institutions.[3]

However, the inner city of Johannesburg also experienced a period of crisis in the late twentieth century. With the intensification of white flight, the inner city saw a deterioration of urban services and infrastructure, as well as low payment levels for rates and services, which were precipitated further by increased outflow of businesses to new office parks in decentralized locations to the north of Johannesburg in the 1980s.[4] Residential development in Johannesburg has subsequently become increasingly balkanized, with settlements proceeding away from the inner city both to the south and the north.[5] Furthermore, most new informal settlements and low-income housing projects are located on cheap land, far away from the city center. Thus, rather than promoting integrated development, the implementation of housing policy in post-apartheid Johannesburg has increased social and spatial exclusion.

On the other hand, the informal sector has had an explosive expansion, especially in areas abandoned by the formal economy.[6] The growth of unregulated street trading represents a response to the far-reaching structural changes in the country's economy, arising from exposure to the global market and a sharp drop in formal employment opportunities.[7]

Thus, in many ways, Johannesburg is becoming more and more like other African cities, as noted by AbdouMaliq Simone when he diagnosed the "wild topographies" of cities like Johannesburg, Lagos, and Douala—in neighborhoods across which urban actors forge a wide range of networks, connections, and global assemblages. Thus, his concept, "People as Infrastructure" emphasizes the economic collaboration among people marginalized from and immiserated by urban life. In these cities, people organize themselves and engage in various heterogeneous activities daily in order to support and sustain their livelihoods. These collaborations enable them not only to survive but also to escape the vicious cycle of poverty and allow for better chances of improved livelihoods. Simone further argues that African cities are continuously flexible, mobile, and provisional intersections of residents that operate without clearly delineated notions of how the city is to be inhabited and used, despite state attempts to control and codify urban space in Johannesburg.

Then again, Johannesburg is also an ordinary city, as noted by Jenny Robinson, who argues against the pathologization of African cities generally and critiques taxonomies of "mega-cities," "World Cities," and "Global Cities" (outlined by Mike Davis, Richard Hall, and Saskia Sassen, respectively). Robinson argues against that division in urbanist literature, whereas development literature usually addresses itself to cities in the "global south"—and urbanist literature—which addresses itself to cities in the so-called "global north." Rather, she says that we should think of cities as ordinary.

Johannesburg *is* an ordinary city, and yet it is important to recognize the historical specificity of colonialism in Johannesburg's morphology—specifically, because the apartheid city was constituted through a thorough reorganization of its urban space for the purposes of racial segregation and labor control. Despite the existence of a large black population, the apartheid policy of "separate development" meant that Africans were only temporarily in the white cities to serve in the mines, work in industries, and provide various services. Until the 1980s Africans, Indians, and other "coloreds" were moved from the city to the urban periphery.

Introduction

The model apartheid city has an exclusively white CBD, surrounded by an extensive consolidated white residential core with freedom to expand into environmentally desirable and accessible sectors in suburban localities. Within this model, socioeconomic patterns in white residential areas remain relatively undisturbed. "Colored" and Indian "group areas," and especially African townships, are located peripherally within given sectors; hostels for migrant workers no longer adjoin the workplace as in the pre-1948 segregation era but were relocated within these townships, which increases the commuter distances and time for the city's racialized others.[8]

In Johannesburg, increased African urbanization between 1933–34 and 1947–48 and the growth of mid-1940s radical African politics heightened white fears about the political dangers of a large African urban population—the *swart gevaar* ("black peril").[9, 10, 11] The National Party victory in 1948 resulted in the steady institutionalization of the racially repressive and segregated political and economic institutions of apartheid.[12] However, this *swart gevaar* was preceded by an earlier one in the 1930s that was marked by a number of "sex panics." Various scholars of South Africa have noted the prevalence of social anxieties about sex and race during a similar period.[13] Sex and race were identified as social problems threatening the fundamental moral fiber and social order of colonial society. This phenomenon was not only concerned with the protection of white civilization from the "pollution" of miscegenation, but it was also preoccupied with policing against the transgressions in sexuality and desire.[14]

Such anxieties created the conditions for new legislation that forbade any boundary crossings, and it was aimed directly at restoring the sexual and social distance necessary for the survival of racial hierarchies in the colonial order.[15] Therefore, race politics and the desires that underlie them suggest, as Jock McCulloch does in *Black Peril, White Virtue*, that jostling for access to power and positioning gender and race in the nascent structure of colonial society were complex and characterized by dynamics between fear and fantasy.

Very often, when historians tell the history of Johannesburg, they begin with the discovery of gold and the ascendency of Johannesburg as the heartland of English capital in South Africa. Understandably, this forms a neat chronology of the city, a "moment zero," which privileges the idea of a single originary moment that passes through the use of modern infrastructure as a tool of racializing socio-technical control under apartheid.[16]

This story also culminates in the victory of the ruling party, the African National Congress (ANC) in 1994—in the first multiracial democratic elections in South Africa, followed by the rapid demise of the inner city, often represented as a "ruin" of modernity brought on by what some urbanists have described as desegregation, or more commonly and particularly problematically, as "graying."[17]

Since its inception in the late nineteenth century as a mining boom town, public health inspectors and police officers were the first public authorities of the city. However, rather than merely reflecting a concern for public order, safety, and health, the discourse of public order in Johannesburg was always imbricated with anxieties surrounding racial and sexual otherness, and a concern for an idealized colonial social order and the hierarchies immanent to that order. This "sanitation syndrome," a term coined by the historian Maynard Swanson, suggested that medical officers and other public authorities in South Africa were imbued with a social imaginary of infectious disease as a social metaphor. Swanson's "sanitation syndrome" demonstrates how the discourse of disease instantiated and legitimized the introduction of urban residential segregation in South African cities at the turn of the century.[18]

This metaphor of infectious disease, like the city itself, has undergone several iterations of destruction, displacement, and reconfiguration, in an attempt to resolve the ongoing contradiction that lies at the core of the city's inception, namely the spatialization, instrumentalization, and disavowal of certain kinds of lived identities and spatial practices, and the inequalities and power asymmetries associated with them. This metaphor of disease was rooted in European and colonial notions of what it meant to be bourgeois. It was defined through a language of difference that drew on images of racial purity and sexual virtue, which distinguished them from populations they deemed "culturally dissonant." Whereas bourgeois bodies were defined as sexually distinguished and cultivated in distinctly racist ways, the figure of the colonized subject was used as a reference point of difference, which served to underscore the dangers of miscegenation and "moral decline." Thus, the discourse on European bourgeois selves and spaces was based on a hierarchy of distinctions in perception and practice that strategically mobilized the categories of racial, class, and sexual others.

This new configuration of a bourgeois "class" body was constituted through the working of race through the language of class. Such discourses on difference not only served the interests of the bourgeois but also lent moral authority to colonialism and nineteenth-century liberal states. Laura Stoler extends Michel Foucault's argument further through her engagement with the coloniality of bourgeois identity thus:

> In the nineteenth century...race becomes the ordering grammar of an imperial order in which modernity, the civilizing mission and the 'measure of man' was framed. And with it, 'culture' was harnessed to do more specific political work; not only to mark difference, but to rationalize the hierarchies of privilege and profit, to consolidate the labour regimes of expanding capitalism, to provide the psychological scaffolding for the exploitative structures of colonial rule.[19]

In addition to securing class interests as noted above, colonial racism also created the conditions for large numbers of the bourgeois and the petty bourgeois to stylize themselves and to enact pseudo-aristocratic fantasies in the colonies, which would otherwise have been inaccessible to them in the city. Whereas this encoding of bourgeois sensibilities with race was transmuted into more subtle scales measuring cultural competency and "suitability," which often replaced explicit racial criteria to define access to privilege in imperial ventures (Stoler, 1985:99), these codes, rather than dissolving within teleological narrative of spatial transformation, reemerge through the respatialization of Johannesburg as a "world-class African City" and the spatial and social violence associated with it.

The work of our own Studio-X Johannesburg recognizes that it is important to understand the materiality of the city rigorously in relation to what Foucault refers to as a certain "grid of intelligibility." However, it also embarks on a slightly different narrative, or set of narratives, about the city's many voices and metamorphoses that not only explore the complexity and kaleidoscopic quality of the metropolitan region of Johannesburg, but will also use those explorations as the basis for a practice of critical enquiry and radical imagination that is rooted in a collective and collaborative rescripting of mutuality—rethinking the possibilities of the city yet to come.

References

Graham, Steven and Simon Marvin. *Splintering Urbanism: Networked Infrastructures, Technological Mobilities and the Urban Condition*. New York: Routledge, 2001.

Mabin, Alan. "The Dynamics of Urbanization since 1960." In Mark Swilling, Richard Humphries and Khehla Shubane (Eds.) *Apartheid City in Transition*. Oxford: Oxford University Press, 1991.

Parnell, Susan and Owen Crankshaw. "Race, Inequality and Urbanisation in the Johannesburg Region, 1946-1996," in Jospeh Gugler (ed.) *World Cities Beyond the West: Globalisation, Development and Inequality*. Cambridge: Cambridge University Press, 2004.

Parnell, Susan. "The politics of transformation: Defining city strategy in Johannesburg," in (ed. K. Segbers) *The Making of Global City Regions: An Exploration of Johannesburg, Mumbai/Bombay, São Paulo, and Shanghai*. Baltimore: John Hopkins Press, 2007.

Robinson, Jennifer. "Global and World Cities: A View From Off the Map" in *International Journal of Urban and Regional Research*, December 16, 2002.

Roy, Anaya. "Urban Informality, Towards an Epistemology of Planning." In *Journal of American Planning Association*, Vol. 71, No. 2, Spring 2005.

Simone, AbduMaliq. "People as Infrastructure." *Public Culture*, 16 (3): 407–29; Duke University Press, 2004.

Stoler, Laura Ann. *Race and the Education of Desire: Foucault's History of Sexuality and the Colonial Order of Things*. Durham, NC: Duke University Press, 1995.

Swanson, Maynard. "Sanitation Syndrome: Bubonic Plague and Urban Native Policy in the Cape Colony, 1900-1909" in *Journal of African History*, xviii (1977), 387–410.

Tissington, Kate. "The Business of Survival: Informal Trading in Inner City Johannesburg" Centre for Applied Legal Studies, 2009.

Tomlinson, Richard, Robert A. Beauregard, Lindsay Bremner and Xolela Mangcu. *Emerging Johannesburg: Perspectives on the Postapartheid City*. New York: Routledge, 2003.

Van Onselen, Charles. *New Babylon, New Nineveh: Everyday Life on the Witwatersrand 1886–1914*. Cape Town: Jonathan Ball, 2001.

Notes

1. Salman Rushdie, *Shalimar the Clown* (New York: Random House, 2006), 5.
2. From Johannesburg Redevelopment Agency: www.jda.org.za.
3. Tomlinson et al, 48.
4. According to Tomlinson, the inner city has 2,151,594 square meters of A- and B-grade office space, including Braamfontein, as proposed to 817,562 square meters in Sandton in 1998.
5. Tomlinson et al, 13. The latter figure declines to 37 percent if Alexandra, the township that withstood forced removal, is deleted from the calculations.
6. The distribution of informal activities shows that 46 percent are in retail, 31 percent in services, and only 23 percent in manufacturing. Families and households can only survive by combining earnings.
7. Tomlinson et al, 49.
8. The Group Areas Acts of 1950 and 1966 intensified the racial segregation set out with the Native Urban Areas Act of 1923. It produced distinctive apartheid cities. Thus, the Group Areas Acts formed the cornerstone of segregated education, health, and social services, and also of local authorities. They exemplify the fundamental

tenet of apartheid ideology, that incompatibility between ethnic groups must be kept to an absolute minimum in order to ensure "harmonious relations," by establishing areas for the exclusive occupation of a given ethnic group. See: Anthony Lemon, "The Apartheid City," in *Homes Apart: South Africa's Segregated Cities* (Capetown: David Phillip Publishers, 1991).

9. Nicolai Nattrass, "Economic Aspects of the Construction of Apartheid, " in Philip Bonner, Peter Delius, and Deborah Posel eds. *Apartheid's Genesis: 1935-1962* (Johannesburg: Ravan Press, 1993).

10. According to Bonner et. al. this paranoia heightened the politicization of racism among the Afrikaner working classes and petite bourgeoisie. Low-wage African labor had long represented a threat to white workers who constituted a sudden and massive redistribution of Afrikaners from the rural areas to larger industrial towns. White workers actively resisted attempts to improve the bargain position of their black counterparts and also enjoyed a modest prosperity in this period. Between 1933 and 1939, white employment in secondary industry increased by 68 percent to 115,000, and these numbers continued to grow during the Second World War. White unemployment was gradually extinguished and with it the poor white problem. During the war years this group was confronted with a number of acute problems such as job competition in secondary industry. Afrikaner workers became a disaffected group who increasingly saw their salvation not with the Labor Party, but with purified nationalists and their promises of racial barriers.

11. Nattrass, 47.

12. See: Oliver C. Philips, "The 'Perils' of Sex and the Panics of Race: The Dangers of Inter-Racial Sex in Colonial Southern Rhodesia," in *African Sexualities: A Reader*, ed. Sylvia Tamale (London: Pambazuka Press, 2011); "Black and White Peril: the 'Perils of Sex' in colonial Zimbabwe," *Journal of Southern African Studies*, 16(4): 669–720; Jock McCullough, *Black Peril, White Virtue, Sexual Crime in Southern Rhodesia, 1902-1935* (Bloomington, University of Indiana Press, 2000).

13. Nattrass, 48.

14. These social anxieties were expressed in the form of lynch mobs and violent retributions against (predominantly lower-class) white women and black men.

15. Graham and Marvin.

16. Simone.

17. Swanson.

18. Stoler, 27.

Shandukani

Kylie Dickson and Henry Paine

Henry Paine is a founding partner of Henry Paine + Partners
Architects in Johannesburg.

Kylie Dickenson is an architect working at Henry Paine + Partners Architects.

VIEW OF THE INSIDE OF THE X-RAY ROOM
(PHOTOGRAPH FOUND AT THE ADLER MUSEUM AT THE
JOHANNESBURG GENERAL HOSPITAL)

Historical Background of the Johannesburg Hospital Site

In 1889, the construction of the first official hospital in Johannesburg commenced on a site that became known as Hospital Hill. Here, patients of all classes were treated without distinction of color, race, or religion. As Johannesburg grew rapidly during the 1890s, so did the hospital. Looking at an historic site plan dated 1932, one notices many new buildings, including temporary wards, a mortuary, laundry, nurses' home and a "natives'"compound.[1]

In 1928, the operating theaters and main X-ray department block were completed.[1] Designed by architect Gordon Leith, it consisted of a two-story structure of beautifully crafted red English bond brickwork. Purple-colored bullnose brick forms the top of the brick plinth, and specially made curved corner bricks appear at the stairways. An elaborate

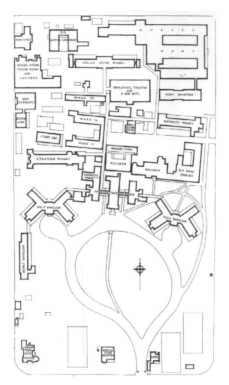

SITE PLAN OF JOHANNESBURG
HOSPITAL, 1932

SOUTHERN FACADE OF BUILDING PRIOR TO CONSTRUCTION.
(PHOTOGRAPHY BY HENRY PAINE)

plaster cornice under the roof eaves articulates the top of the concrete roof slab and assists in carrying the shaped brackets that support the secondary hipped roof of corrugated iron (this double-roof was a device that helped keep the building cool). Three prominent surgical theaters define the form of the building's southern facade, and with their external staircases emphasize the relationship between the hospital and the university (students could enter the theaters' viewing galleries without entering the building proper).

The demands placed on the hospital resulted in eighty years of ad hoc additions to the hospital site (resulting in an illegible layout of buildings) and to the X-ray building itself. The brickwork reveals additions that were made to the second floor as well as to the lift shaft; a double-story electrical substation was attached to the northern facade; a laundry building with chute was attached to the eastern facade; new, poorly constructed flat composite roofs were built on the second-floor additions, and much of the original S-profile corrugated iron replaced with industrial roof sheeting.

The Closure of the Johannesburg Health Precinct

Hillbrow used to be the most trendy and cosmopolitan area in Johannesburg; today it is thought to be one of the most tightly packed places on the continent. Immigrants and migrants from the rest of the country and the continent head for Hillbrow's crowded anonymity and informal economy as a first stop on the way to finding employment and accommodation—over half its inhabitants are believed to be refugees, whether legal or illegal... The result is a highly transient, fragmented, poverty-stricken population, speaking a multitude of languages and living in an area renowned for its many sex workers and high levels of drugs and crime... health care workers say about 30 percent of the adult population is HIV-positive.[3]

Johannesburg's new General Hospital was built in 1983, on the outskirts of the city center, across the motorway. From this point onward the Hillbrow

Shandukani

Hospital (formerly Johannesburg Hospital) became less relevant as departments, staff, and equipment moved across to the new facility. In 1997 the surgical theaters and X-ray building were officially abandoned by the government. The window openings were bricked up and doors placed under lock and key—another nail in the coffin for the declining suburb of Hillbrow.

Breathing New Life Into Hillbrow

WrHI (Wits Reproductive Health Institute)—formerly RHRU—was formed in 1994 to provide the newly elected democratic government with technical support for health policy formulation and to develop a relevant research agenda in the field of reproductive health.[4]

WrHI's head office is located in the heart of Hillbrow within the Hillbrow Health Precinct. Being located there, it is able to directly influence issues such as poverty, HIV, urban decay, and, most importantly, primary health care, which is accessible to the local community that so desperately needs it. These head offices are located within the recently renovated Hugh Solomon Building (formerly the nurses' home), with almost direct access to Shandukani.

Funded by three companies (Vodacom, Altron, and Altech), supported by the Gauteng Department of Health as well as the city of Johannesburg, and facilitated by WrHI, Shandukani (a Venda word meaning "change" or "asking for change") was set to become a reality.

The Design Rationale

We, as the architects, were asked to adapt the old operating theater and X-ray building into prenatal and antenatal facilities that were to be operated by the Department of Health as well as a research center to be run by WrHI.

We were asked to design "a 'happy place' with unintimidating materials, finishes, and furnishings; that is, it should be more like a living room than

Dickson / Paine

GROUND FLOOR OF BUILDING PRIOR TO CONSTRUCTION
(PHOTOGRAPH: ROGER BULL)

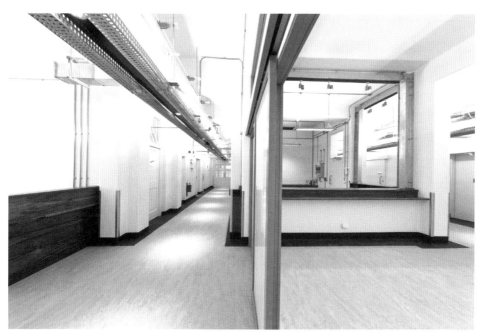

GROUND FLOOR AFTER CONSTRUCTION
(PHOTOGRAPH: ROGER BULL)

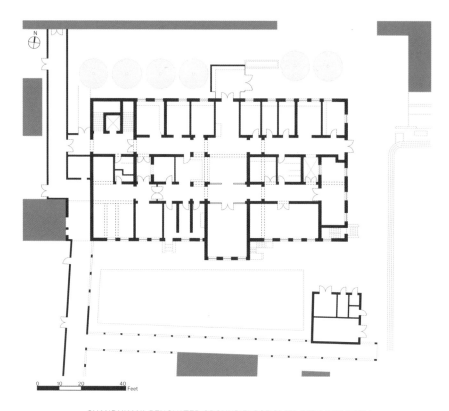

SHANDUKANI, RENOVATED GROUND FLOOR PLAN. REDRAWN FROM
HENRY PAINE AND PARTNERS ARCHITECTS, 2012.

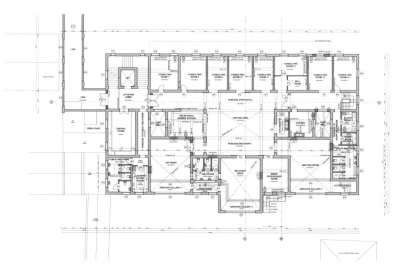

FIRST FLOOR PLAN

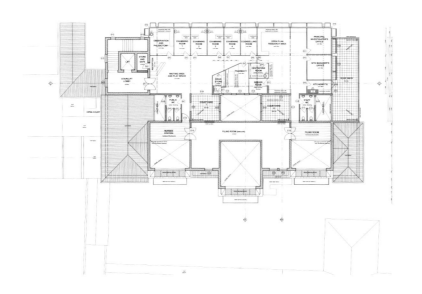

SECOND FLOOR PLAN

PERSPECTIVE FROM THE NORTHEAST

43

Shandukani

a hospital." The spaces were to be designed to be comfortable for mothers and children as well as for the staff who were to occupy it.

Heritage and Conservation

The well-known architect Gordon Leith designed many of the buildings of what is, arguably, the best collection of conservation-worthy buildings in Johannesburg, making up the Hillbrow Health Precinct. The two-story load-bearing brick building was opened in 1928 as "one of the most advanced operating theaters in the Union."

The building was adapted according to the maxim of doing "as much as necessary and as little as possible to the building." As the main building had been abandoned for many years, it had become severely damaged and waterlogged, resulting in the need for a complete overhaul, which necessitated an extensive refit of services as well as the addition of new services required by modern medicine.

The building was not large enough to accommodate all the needs of the new facility, and it was necessary to add a third floor over a conveniently located flat-roofed area on the north side of the building. It is possible that an extension over this area was envisaged by Leith in 1927.

As heritage practitioners, it was clear to us that a comparatively lightweight structure would be needed to form new accommodation on the existing flat roof. The new structure had to have minimal impact on the original structure, and it had to be possible to remove it and return the building to its original configuration if this should be required in the future. The ability to return a building to an earlier/original period is an important heritage principle. The structure had to be quickly and easily erected in a densely packed precinct surrounded by buildings that were already occupied. The conservation-related reason of adding to the building in a way that clearly differentiated "new" from "old" reinforced the rationale. The floor area of the new third floor needed to be larger than the existing roof, necessitating a cantilevered extension over the north façade.

SOUTH FACADE AFTER CONSTRUCTION: SHOWING VIEWING
GALLERIES TO SURGICAL THEATERS
(PHOTOGRAPH: ROGER BULL)

NORTH FACADE AFTER CONSTRUCTION
(PHOTOGRAPH: KYLIE DICKSON)

Shandukani

The aesthetic of the building is entirely determined by needs and by the natural characteristics of the materials used (predominantly steel and glass). The new structure was intended to contrast with the original brick building and to provide sun protection for the floor below. The lightweight steel roof was insulated and overhangs the windows to give protection from the summer sun. A lightweight grille also provides privacy from an existing building to the north and supplements protection from sun and glare.

The building is not air conditioned, a decision made from the point of view of sustainability as well as for medical reasons. Infection and particularly (tuberculosis) control requires maximum natural ventilation and a continuous supply of fresh air, not recycled air, as is the case with air conditioning. Further, the client expressed a strong preference for natural ventilation through opening windows to create a pleasant working environment. The new, steel-framed part of the building has been designed with sun protection and insulation that will make air conditioning unnecessary; the old parts of the building were designed by Gordon Leith to be cool in summer. Ventilation and heating (when temperatures make it necessary) are provided by a system that allows for adjustment of airflow volume and temperature.

Sustainability (Green Architecture)

Environmental concerns were paramount in the design of the building. Eighty percent of the new steel structure can be recycled, and the entire old structure has been recycled in ways that are sustainable. Should circumstances change at some point, the use of steel makes it possible to dismantle the structure, reuse it, and leave the building in its original state. Considering the issues of recycling and those of climate control with minimal use of new materials, it would be very difficult to design a building with a smaller carbon footprint than Shandukani.

Conclusion

As the architects of the project, we would like to thank our team of professionals as well as the contractors for all the work they have

Dickson / Paine

dedicated to this initiative. Special thanks are due to the sponsors of the project: Vodacom, Altron, and Altech and to the client WrHI, represented by Yael Horowitz.

References

Bruwer, J.J. "Heritage Assessment for the Proposed Renovation and Adaptive Reuse of Building" (47). September, 2010.

Schreiber, Lorna. Johannesburg Hospital/ Hospitaal, 1890-1990. Johannesburg: Johannesburg Hospital Board, 1990.

"South Africa: Hospital Project Attempts to Revive Johannesburg Inner City." *IRIN Humanitarian News and Analysis*. May 14, 2010.

Horowitz, Y. RHRH Background Document—RHRH Hillbrow Health Precinct and Center for Specialised Services. 2010.

Shandukani

Jo'burg

Guy Tillim

Guy Tillim is a photographer working in South Africa. His photography documents projects of visual and historical strength to create testimonies to the social conflict and inequalities prevailing in South Africa.

Introduction by John Barrett

The high-rise apartment blocks of Hillbrow are open books to the streetwise. Their facades, in varying degrees of disrepair, reveal volumes. In a nation of eleven official languages, they speak to the common experience of millions of hopeful residents from all of Africa, Southern Asia, and Europe who have sought better lives in Hillbrow. Starting in the 1970s, Hillbrow evolved from a territory of speculation and segregation into vibrant integration, then evacuation, immigration, and episodic expulsion. Perhaps no area of Johannesburg is as clearly physically inscribed with the burdens, guilt, and hope of the entire nation.

Built in a spasm of speculative development in the twilight of the apartheid regime, Hillbrow was originally conceived as a cosmopolitan, residential enclave for the white professional class in the 1970s. Demand from white South Africans never materialized and Hillbrow's building owners began overlooking segregation laws and admitting non-whites. For a short time these market forces produced a flourishing neighborhood of unique racial diversity, and in fact the neighborhood was referred to admiringly as the Manhattan of Johannesburg. In the final years of the apartheid state whites began to flee the inner city. By the time of the democratic elections of 1994, the neighborhood had largely become an overcrowded slum—a condition that has persisted unabated.

The paradox of Hillbrow today is that while the neighborhood continues to grapple with some of the most acute stresses of urban life in Africa, it remains a beacon of opportunity for millions of immigrants seeking better lives. The most vulnerable residents live their daily lives with physical hardship and deep insecurity perpetuated by what is functionally a failed state at the scale of a very dense neighborhood. Hillbrow today has a density similar to that of Manhattan, about 100,000 residents from every nation in Southern Africa living in 1.5 square kilometers of central Jo'burg. The civil infrastructures of water supply, trash collection, and municipal sewers remain broken and overwhelmed while absentee landlords neglect tax bills. The ineffective and corrupt JMPD provides little public security for the residents, who are forced to band together to hire private security guards to selectively police areas that can afford their fees. In the interest of minimizing violence, the private security forces maintain a truce with local power brokers, allowing drug dealing, prostitution, and the attendant assaults on public health to flourish. Residents live in overcrowded, uncomfortable, dark, and unsafe housing blocks of ten to twenty stories, many with largely broken facades and without functional elevators or fire safety systems. The lack of security creates situations in which some buildings are controlled by gangs who siphon rent from powerless immigrant residents. When an owner decides to retake his property, these residents are often thrown out on the street with no warning or recourse.

Jo'burg

AL'S TOWER, A BLOCK OF FLATS ON HARROW ROAD,
BEREA, OVERLOOKING THE PONTE BUILDING,
GUY TILLIM, JO'BURG, 2004

SAN JOSE, A BLOCK OF FLATS ON OLIVIA STREET, BEREA,
GUY TILLIM, JO'BURG, 2004

The City Council has instituted proceedings against the tenants with the intention to evict on the grounds that the building is unhygienic and a fire hazard. This legislation, under the Building Regulations Act, does not require the city to provide alternative accommodation.

ON THE ROOF OF JEANWELL HOUSE ON NUGGET STREET,
GUY TILLIM, JO'BURG, 2004

Electricity and water supplies to Jeanwell have been cut off since September 2003.
The residents are in negotiation with the owner about maintenance of the building
and have ceased to pay rent.

TAYOB TOWERS, PRITCHARD STREET,
GUY TILLIM, JO'BURG, 2004

MEMBERS OF WOZANI SECURITY, KNOWN AS THE RED ANTS,
ENTER THE CHELSEA HOTEL IN HILLBROW DURING A CLEANUP OPERATION,
GUY TILLIM, JO'BURG, 2004

The residents were evicted some months earlier.

EVICTION AFTERMATH, NOVERNA COURT, PAUL NEL STREET, HILLBROW,
GUY TILLIM, JO'BURG, 2004

Geological Health

Lindsay Bremner

Dr. Lindsay Bremner is Director of Architectural Research at the University of Westminster in London. She was previously the head of architecture departments at Temple University in Philadelphia and the University of Witwatersrand in Johannesburg. She is an award-winning architect and writer on Johannesburg, including the book *Writing the City into Being: Essays on Johannesburg 1998–2008* (2010).

We forget or choose to ignore that when humans turn the earth inside out, it is inevitable that health consequences follow. Throughout history, mining and its aftermath have had staggering, politically inflected consequences for the health of human and nonhuman life. On the Witwatersrand, where the underground and the aboveground are entwined in intimate flows of geological, biological, economic, and sociopolitical life, its effects are particularly potent.

Mine Boy is one of the earliest mining novels by a black South African writer. In it, a picture of underground life and of the intimacy between geology and the body emerges:

> The men were silent. It was always so. Going into the bowels of the earth forced silence on them. And their hearts pounded. Many had gone in day after day for months. But they did not get used to it. Always there was the furious pounding of the hearts. The tightness in the throat. And the warm feeling in the belly.[1]

The underground, for the miner, was palpable, visceral, felt in the body, and often resulted in sudden, or slow, invisible death. Xuma, the boss boy in *Mine Boy*, is a rural peasant who comes to Johannesburg to find work. A shebeen owner, Leah, takes him in and asks him where he will work. "On the mines," he replies. To which she responds, "The mines are no good, Xuma, later on you cough and then you spit blood and you become weak and die. I have seen it many times. To-day you are young and you are strong, and to-morrow you are thin and ready to die . . ."[2]

Leah is here describing the path through the body taken by silicosis and its resulting pulmonary tuberculosis. They are the primary occupational diseases of gold mining, the consequence of drilling, blasting, and grinding at rock faces with a high silica content to produce the ore from which gold is extracted. This releases dust, which, when inhaled over long periods, results in silicosis, often leading to tuberculosis or lung cancer. A recent book by Jock McCulloch gives an account of the system of racialized medicine delivered by mining companies in South Africa to treat these diseases throughout the apartheid years. White workers were relatively well-treated and compensated, while black workers, mostly employed as migrant labor on short-term contracts, were repatriated once they became ill, exporting what McCullough calls a "tide of disease" to rural areas and neighboring countries, with enormous ongoing social and economic costs.[3]

On the Witwatersrand, the world's richest goldfields, gold is found, along with uranium, carbon, and pyrite in a fractured, dense formation of underground layers, seams, and faults (figure 1). The gold appears as veinlets, specks, or grains in the cracks and cavities of layers of carbonaceous conglomerate. This layer can be anything from a centimeter to more than a meter thick and slope at an angle of twenty degrees or more toward the south to depths of at least 5,000 meters. It surfaces in a 3-kilometer-wide belt from 65 kilometers east of Johannesburg to 145 kilometers west of the city, and then again in the Orange Free State, 320 kilometers to the southwest.

This underground configuration has had profound consequences for the towns and cities that sprung up above to exploit it. Early miners found gold ore close to the surface in long outcrops, known as reefs, running east to west along the valley floor. These were mined in shallow trenches but soon exhausted. Accessing the deeper strata of conglomerate required sinking inclined shafts, horizontal tunnels, raises, and stopes to extract the sloping gold seam as it fell sharply away. This is illustrated in a sectional drawing through a mining operation drawn in 1897 (figure 2). As a consequence of this geometry of shafts and tunnels, the earth's geological strata were weakened and in constant danger of collapsing

63

(figure 3). All that could be constructed over them were lightweight industrial buildings or the tailings of mining operations, colloquially known as mine dumps. Johannesburg and other mining towns were laid out to the north of the initial line of diggings, not only to avoid collapses and sinkholes but also to evade the mine dust blown off the dumps by the prevailing northeast or northwest winds. The southern industrial extremities of the towns butted up against or were threaded through the metallurgical landscape of mining headgear, battery stamps, reduction works, ore dumps, mine dumps, slimes dams, railways, and vacant land.

Early Johannesburg was crisscrossed by a number of small watercourses, the biggest of which formed a swampy hollow to the west of the city. Here, the poorest inhabitants lived in what were known as the Kaffir and Coolie locations (figure 4). In 1904, pneumonic plague broke out in the Coolie location. It was cordoned off, evacuated, and burned to the ground, and its entire population of more than 3,000 people relocated to Klipspruit, an area 20 kilometers to the southwest of the city. This was the first displacement of the city from the north to the south of the gold mines and set the pattern for the subsequent racial reorganization of the urban territory. After the proclamation of the Black Urban Areas Act in 1924, the city of Johannesburg proper became increasingly white, while more and more black people were forcibly removed and relocated to the black dormitory city of Soweto to the southwest. The mining belt, governed separately from the city, served as a negative zone, cutting a great swath between the two.[4]

Since the 1970s, large-scale adjustments in the gold mining industry and to gold's status in the global financial system have resulted in mine closures, mine abandonment, or changes of ownership in this central part of the Witwatersrand. Mining operations, buildings, machinery, and land lying close to the city center became valuable resources for a number of other economies: second-tier mining companies or artisanal miners have taken over defunct mining property; mining headgear and plants have been scavenged for their scrap metals; dumps have been reprocessed to remove traces of gold and release their land for real estate speculation; residue has been pumped hydrologically to gigantic new super dumps

MINE LANDSCAPES, 2009-2012
(PHOTOGRAPHS: LINDSAY BREMNER)

Geological Health

farther from the city; and, given the paradox of lying at the center of the urban system but outside of municipal jurisdiction and being too contaminated for development, vacant mining land has been settled by the urban poor. Today, there are at least 400,000 of the poorest of people living in informal settlements on this land.[5]

But this earth is far from dormant, hospitable, or healthy. It is riddled with deep shafts, underground tunnels, mine dumps, waste rock dumps, open cast excavations, quarries, water storage facilities, dams, tailings spillage sites, and general unauthorized urban waste. Having been tunneled into, excavated, blasted, pumped, transmuted, discarded, and dumped, the earth is literally buzzing with life. Its topographies, hydrologies, and ecologies are adjusting to and recomposing the structural, chemical, and radiological aftereffects of mining. It is less of an environment than what Jane Bennett calls a "vital materiality"—an unstable, entangled, emergent geo-bio-chemico-radiological-social system, and a highly toxic one at that.

The first thing one notices about Witwatersrand is that it leads a highly volatile structural life. It is under-mined by an extensive, invisible underground network of interconnected tunnels and sloping mining voids propped up by reef pillars, wooden supports, and buried infrastructure. Once mining operations ceased, this underground void was simply abandoned. It is geotechnically unstable and prone to unpredictable cavings-in and collapses, which crack or fissure the earth, mine dumps, building foundations, floors, and walls above it. Its frequently occurring unsealed, unprotected surface openings and ventilation shafts provide passageways in and out of the earth for percolating water, air, animals, and people. These include informal settlers and artisanal miners, whose precarious lives often end tragically.

The mine dumps remaining on the land are an arsenal of radioactivity and heavy metals. They contain vast quantities of uranium and the iron-sulphide pyrite, also known as fool's gold (FeS_2).[6] Neither of these are in themselves threatening, but when they come into contact with air and water and interact with each other, toxic chemical chain reactions

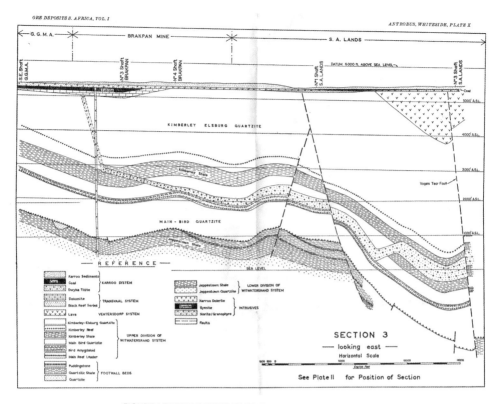

FIGURE 1: SECTION THROUGH THE MINING BELT IN THE EAST RAND
SHOWING UNDERGROUND LAYERS, SEAMS FAULTS AND GOLD SEAMS
SOURCE: SYDNEY H. HAUGHTON, THE GEOLOGY OF SOME ORE DEPOSITS
IN SOUTH AFRICA (1964)

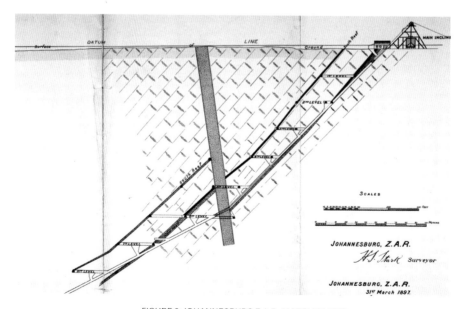

FIGURE 2: JOHANNESBURG Z.A.R., MARCH 31, 1897
CROSS SECTION THROUGH A TYPICAL GOLD MINE

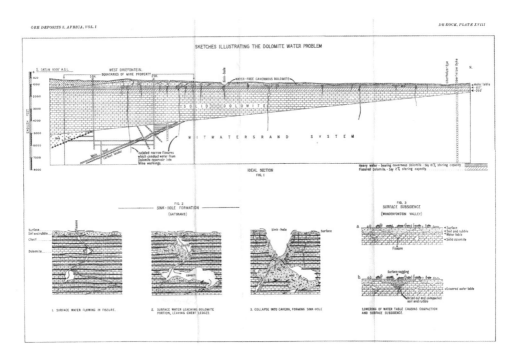

FIGURE 3: SKETCHES SHOWING THE DANGERS OF SURFACE COLLAPSE
WHEN UNDERGROUND WATER LEVELS ARE TAMPERED WITH BY MINING
SOURCE: SYDNEY H. HAUGHTON, THE GEOLOGY OF SOME ORE DEPOSITS
IN SOUTH AFRICA (1964)

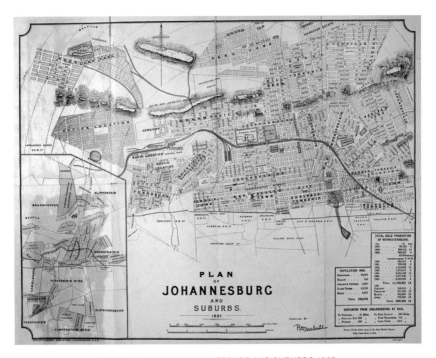

FIGURE 4: PLAN OF JOHANNESBURG AND SUBURBS, 1897
THE KAFIR AND COOLIE LOCATIONS CAN BE SEEN IN THE
SOUTHWEST CORNER OF THE CITY

result. Water scientist Anthony Turton has broken these interactions down into a number of sequences, each with a fundamentally different set of cause-effect linkages.[7] They are set in motion by the fall of acid rain on an alkaline, pyrite-rich mine dump. This lowers the pH level on the surface and triggers the release of hydrogen, fueling an acidification process. Pyrite (FeS_2) oxidizes in the presence of air and water to form an acidic solution of ferrous iron and sulphate. Ferrous iron then oxidizes to ferric iron, and ferric iron then precipitates as ferric hydroxide, producing further acidification.[8] The resulting water has a low pH (sometimes as low as 3.0), a high concentration of dissolved salts (mostly sulphates), high electrical conductivity, and mobilizes elevated levels of heavy metals, depending on the host geology it has flowed through. The seepage of this water out of surface dumps and into wetlands alters the electrical conductivity of the earth. This makes underground infrastructures using cathode protection particularly vulnerable to corrosion when close to high-voltage power lines, caused by electromagnetic forces operating under different parameters. Typical manifestations of acid mine drainage also result in anoxic conditions (the absence of free oxygen), hence the killing off of biological life that can only survive under aerobic conditions. Once the pH of a mine tailing is lowered to 5.0 in this process, uranium starts to be leached out, at rates that depend on oxic/anoxic conditions.[9] The oxidized uranium is concentrated in the crust of the dump and, mobilized by wind and rain, is distributed over the landscape and into rivers and wetlands. As it is dissolved by acid mine drainage, its radioactive progeny are mobilized, posing as much of a radiological threat as uranium itself. But uranium and its progeny are not the only radioactive actants here. Radon gas, an odorless, colorless, tasteless, chemically inert gas, is released when uranium-rich dumps are disturbed or re-mined non-hydrolocally. It is heavier than air and sinks into valleys and depressions in the landscape, decaying via alpha particle emission, with a half-life of 3.8 days. This produces progeny with life spans of between 0.2 millionths of a second and 26.8 minutes. Despite their short lives, charged progeny can attach to air particles and are a known cause of lung cancer.

When humans and animals are added to this assemblage, their bodies become sinks for the toxic chemistry unfolding around them. For the nearly half-million people living among this vibrant alchemy, geology is indistinguishable from biology. People inhale airborne radon gas and dust; in some cases, they eat the toxic soil, believing that it relieves stomach pains, or use it as a skin cream; people grow crops on tailings and irrigate them with water packed with radionuclides and chemotoxic metals; these bio-accumulate heavy metals, which, ingested over long periods of time have carcinogenic effects; the internal organs of animals feeding on grass growing close to tailings seepages are contaminated with uranium and cobalt; children play in the dirt and fall into open shafts; simply by living on or close to mine dumps, people are exposed to elevated levels of direct external gamma radiation. In the Tudor Shaft informal settlement on the West Rand, for instance, levels of toxicity are higher than in the Chernobyl exclusion zone. The slow, violent consequences of these exposures are largely invisible and will unfold over many years, even generations. But what is known is that the adults, children, and animals who live in the contaminated zone will be vulnerable to respiratory diseases, cancer, decreased cognitive function, skin lesions, and health risks from internal irradiation, which include neurological illnesses, diabetes, and heart disease.

This is clearly an instance of geology asserting its time and agency. We are no longer in charge. When turned inside out and upside down by humans for short-term economic gain, geology is beginning to reassert itself. To respond and work with it will require acknowledging the intimacy of geo-social relations of the humans and nonhumans in the mix.

Notes

1. Abrahams and Yudelowitz, 147.
2. Ibid, 16.
3. These are still subject to major class actions for compensation (see Prinsloo, 2009).
4. Tang and Watkins.
5. Mining land in South Africa is "proclaimed" once precious metals are discovered. This divests the owner and invests the central state not with ownership but with control over the surface of the land and its gold workings. Licensing provisions then entitle it to grant mining title or mineral rights to third parties to mine. It is not subject to municipal legislation, zoning, servicing, or policing (see Bremner, 2013).
6. Typically, uranium occurs in the earth's crust in quantities of two to four parts per million (grams per ton). Between 1952 and 1988 during production on the Far West Rand, it was measured at 145 grams per ton, with averages elsewhere of between 51 and 383 grams per ton. Witwatersrand mine dumps contain approximately 430,000 tons of low-grade uranium (GDARD, 2011).
7. This counters the argument that acid mine water is created underground in abandoned mine shafts and tunnels (as argued for instance in McCarthy 2010), proposing instead that it is generated on surface mine tailings and seeps into open shafts, slowly rising when pumps are turned off.

Bremner

8. Mine dumps are deposited with a high alkaline content (pH 10.5) because this is the required metallurgical condition for the extraction of gold. Current research suggests that the oxidization of pyrite in these dumps is accelerated by the fall of acid rain, sometimes with a pH value of 3.0. This acidifies the surface of the dump, and the chemistry of acid mine drainage kicks in as follows: Pyrite (FeS_2) oxidizes in the presence of air and water to form an acidic solution of ferrous iron and sulphate. This is chemically described as follows: $4FeS_2 (s) + 14O_2 (g) + 4H_2O = 4Fe^{2+} (aq) + 8SO_4^{2-} (aq) + 8H+ (aq)$, where (s = solid; l = liquid; g = gas; aq = aqueous). This is what happens on the surface of mine dumps when they are exposed to rain water. Ferrous iron ($4Fe^{2+}$) then oxidizes to ferric iron as follows when the acidic water leaves the tailings pile: $4Fe^{2+} (aq) + O_2 (g) + 4H+ (aq) = 4Fe^{3+} (aq) + 2H_2O (l)$. Ferric iron then precipitates as ferric hydroxide, producing further acid, when the acid water enters a local wetland or river as follows: $4Fe^{3+} (aq) + 12H_2O (l) = 4Fe(OH)_3 (s) + 12H+ (aq)$ (Turton, 2013).

9. Exposed to the air, uranium oxidizes, manifesting mostly as triuranium octoxide (U^3O^8) and uranium dioxide (UO^2). These forms of uranium are soluble in water, contingent upon the pH level of the water and the oxic/anoxic state of the water. Some types of uranium dissolve in water with a high pH level, typically containing carbonates, but the same is true for water with a low pH level, containing sulphates, often in the form of sulphuric acid to which uranium is highly susceptible. What this means is that uranium is dissolved in water with pH levels less than 5.0 and greater than 10.0 (Turton, 2013).

References

Abrahams, Peter and Ruth Yudelowitz. *Mine Boy*. London: Heinemann, 1963.

Bega, Sheeree. "Living in South Africa's Own Chernobyl." *Saturday Star*. January 8, 2011.

Bennett, Jane. *Vibrant Matter: A Political Ecology of Things*. Durham: Duke University Press, 2010.

Bremner, Lindsay. "The Politics of Rising Acid Mine Water." *Urban Forum* 24(4), 2013.

Bremner, Lindsay. "Remaking Johannesburg." *Future City*, edited by Steven Read, Jurgen Rosemann and Job van Eldijk. London: Spon, 2005.

Decommissioning Projects—South Africa. "Study finds extreme uranium and heavy metal contamination in cattle grazing near Wonderfontein Spruit." *Wise Uranium Project*. December 18, 2012. http://www. wise-uranium.org/udza.html

Dugard, Jackie, Jennifer MacLeod, and Anna Alcaro. "Rights Mobilization in South Africa in the context of acute environmental harm: The case of Acid Mine Drainage on the Witwatersrand Basin." Paper presented at the Human Rights and the Global Economy Conference at the Center for Public Scholarship, November 9–10, 2011. The New School, New York.

Gauteng Department of Agricultural and Rural Development (GDARD). *Feasibility Study on Reclamation of Mine Residue Areas for Development Purposes: Phase II Strategy and Implementation Plan*, 2011.

Haughton, S.H. *The Geology of Some Ore Deposits in South Africa*. Johannesburg: The Geological Society of South Africa, 1964.

McCarthy, Terrence. The Decanting of Acid Mine Water in the Gauteng City-region: Analysis, Prognosis and Solutions. Provocations Series. Johannesburg: Gauteng City-Region Observatory, 2010.

McCullough, Jock. *South Africa's Gold Mines and the Politics of Silicosis*. Cape Town: Jacan, 2012. Prinsloo, Loni. "Silicosis-stricken ex-miners blame Anglo for their condition, take mining giant to court." *Creamer Media's Mining Weekly*, November 27, 2009. http://www.miningweekly.com/article/ ex-miners-accuses-mining-giant-anglo-of-negli- gence-2009-11-27

Tang, Dorothy and Andrew Watkins. "Ecologies of Gold: Mining Johannesburg Landscapes." *Places*. February 24, 2011. http://places.designobserver. com/slideshow.html?view=1618&entry=25008&sl ide=1

Turton, Anthony. "Debunking Persistent Myths About AMD in the Quest for a Sustainable Solution." *SAWEF Paradigm Shifter* No. 1, 2013. http://www. sawef.co.za/AMD.pdf

Geological Health

Stress

Sandro Galea

Sandro Galea, MD, MPH, DrPH, is Dean of the School of Public Health at Boston University.

Most people will experience some transient reactions, which we typically call "stress," when faced with adversity. These reactions can range from the mild—annoyance, irritation—to the more troublesome, including sleeplessness, nightmares, or explicit efforts to avoid the source of the adversity, the "stressor." In a minority of people, these stress reactions can persist for weeks, months, or years. Increasingly, we are recognizing that a wide range of adverse experiences can cause stress throughout the life span. Poor social conditions, including low-quality urban environments, can cause stress, as can interpersonal experiences such as the death of loved ones, or other extreme traumatic events, such as assault or a motor vehicle accident. Post-traumatic stress disorder is a pathologic condition that represents a long-term stress reaction to a broad range of extreme traumatic events. Stress reactions, from the mild and transient to the long-term and pathological, represent neurobiological changes that, while initially potentially adaptive, become burdensome and maladaptive in the longer term.

Stress, in the urban context and in health terms, can be a misnomer. For architects, stress is measurable and quantified. It's the degree to which a building can bear load, a force that pushes a material to the limits of its capacity. In health, stress is more slippery. It is neither a symptom nor a cause, or it is both. Instead of relying on stress as a catch-all term, it is important for health experts and urban experts to identify those things that may induce stress reactions or be caused by it. In the urban environment, this may be overcrowding and poor housing, contamination from industry or inadequate infrastructure, or a lack of mobility. It might also manifest in an absence of space and resources for healing—both physical and psychological. In Johannesburg, a history of oppression and stark inequality has created urban expanses, that, while culturally and socially rich, are overburdened in regard to their infrastructure and buildings. Coupled with the environmental realities of these areas—places where the climate can exacerbate infection and industry has left toxic traces— the social and material conditions of the city can contribute to illness and mental duress. A precise understanding of stress in the overlap of architecture and public health is integral to understanding how to better serve neighborhoods in Johannesburg and cities globally.

Baragwanath Hospital Buildings: A Brief History

Simonne J. Horwitz

Dr. Simonne J. Horwitz is assistant professor in the Department of History,
University of Saskatchewan in Canada and author of *Baragwanath Hospital,
Soweto: A History of Medical Care 1941-1990.*

In the late nineteenth century Cornish immigrant John Albert
Baragwanath purchased a piece of land one day's journey by ox wagon
from Johannesburg, at the point where the road to Kimberly joined the
road from Vereeniging. Here, Baragwanath set up a refreshment post,
store, and hotel, which were ideally placed to service the flow of travel-
ers, prospectors, and traders who came to seek their fortunes on the
Witwatersrand in the wake of the discovery of gold and diamonds.[1] In the
early twentieth century Baragwanath's land was bought by the Corner
House Mining Group and later taken over by Crown Mines Ltd. but was
never mined. This was the land on which Baragwanath Hospital, the
largest specialist hospital in the Southern Hemisphere came to stand. Its
location, development, and architecture are all products of its multilay-
ered, and sometimes contentious, history.

Two parallel yet intertwined processes led to the establishment of
the hospital on the Baragwanath site in the early 1940s: the need for
a military hospital to serve allied troops, and the longer-term need
for a hospital to serve the expanding urban African population of
the Witwatersrand. In 1939, Britain—and indeed the entire British
Empire—was suffering from backlogs in the provision of health care for
military personnel. As hostilities escalated in the early 1940s, the need
for additional hospitals and convalescent facilities became urgent.[2]
Despite its distance from the front, South Africa was considered a suitable location for additional hospital accommodation for Imperial troops
because of its strategic position and sophisticated medical system.[3] Sir
Edward Thornton, South Africa's secretary of Public Health (1932–8)
and director-general of Medical Services, was said to have advised that

one hospital and depot should be built in Port Elizabeth and another near Johannesburg.[4] While Thornton's suggestion of Port Elizabeth, a coastal town accessible by ship, was considered, only one hospital—in Johannesburg—was ultimately built. Johannesburg was on a main railway line and had a well-developed health infrastructure with a university medical facility that had been in operation since 1922. It offered a climate ideal for recovery of those suffering from diseases like tuberculosis. That it was free of tropical diseases like malaria offered further advantages. In addition, it had nurses' training colleges and rehabilitation facilities. Once it was decided that the hospital was to be built near Johannesburg, military and health officials of both the British and Union Governments entered into a series of consultations.

Throughout the 1940s there was an increasing awareness, at least among some officials within the Union Government, of the desperate need for hospital care for the urban African population. A series of reports, letters, and press articles put increasing pressure on the national and provincial authorities to make improvements to the health care facilities available to urban Africans.[5] It was amid these debates that discussions around the establishment of a military hospital near Johannesburg became intertwined with concurrent debates about urban African health care. As these negotiations began, South Africa was entering a period during which there was not only a slightly more liberal government in power but also a staff of markedly progressive individuals overseeing health care.[6] This opened up a window of opportunity in which a hospital could be built that would serve the military during the war and could then be converted into a civilian hospital at a fraction of the cost of building a new hospital. This set of considerations shaped debates about the location and building of the hospital, which would ultimately be called Baragwanath Hospital.

The Union Government insisted that the hospital be built in a region where it could be converted into a civilian hospital at the end of the war.[7] The Johannesburg Municipality and the Department of Public Works examined a number of sites, all of which were in close proximity to the Baragwanath aerodrome, which had been Johannesburg's leading air

Baragwanath Hospital Buildings

force facility since 1919.[8] This also happened to be in the vicinity of the developing townships of Orlando and Pimville, which would become Soweto.[9] Three sites were considered.

Sites A and B were on council-owned land, while the third site was not. Site B was situated between the two railway lines in the vicinity of Nancefield Station and between the Pimville and Orlando locations. This meant it would be an excellent location for an African hospital after the war. However, the location was the site's only advantage. Not only was it too small for the proposed 1,600-bed hospital, but it was also waterlogged due to the distribution of sewerage effluent over the area—hardly the ideal location for a hospital. At the same time, the clay-rich subsoil made an unsuitable foundation for buildings. Site A, on the other side of the railway line from site B, appeared to be just as waterlogged. The sites could not be joined to solve the size problem, and both seemed unusable.[10] The third site, situated on high ground nearer to the entrance of Orlando, was accessible and had relatively dry soil that would hold the foundations of a large-scale building. However, the council did not own this land; rather it was the piece of land bought by John Albert Baragwanath in the late 1880s that was now in the hands of Crown Mines Ltd. Negotiations were immediately entered into with the mining company, which sold a 100-acre portion of ground to the Union Government, which in turn granted it to the British Government, rent-free, for the duration of the war.[11] By late 1941, as things continued to look bleak for the Allies, there was an urgent need to construct the hospital as quickly as possible. In November 1941 construction started under the auspices of the Red Cross.[12] The Johannesburg Municipality contributed water, electrical, and sewerage services, and it agreed to construct roads and paths within the site at a minimal profit.[13]

In May 1942, seven months after construction began, the Imperial Military Hospital Baragwanath was ready to admit its first patients. The entire facility was complete within eighteen months. The speed of construction was achieved by the employment of several contractors simultaneously.[14]

The style in which the hospital was built bears the marks of its dual purpose. Unlike many military hospitals in South Africa at the time, which consisted either of hutments in existing barracks or under canvas, Baragwanath was planned by the Department of Public Works to be a permanent structure, which greatly increased the costs. Yet, despite the envisioned use of the facility as a civilian hospital after the war, its layout was military in design. It was built in the Pavilion architectural style that had been popular in Britain from the 1850s until the late 1930s.[15] The buildings were originally designed for convalescent patients and were barrack-like, single-story pavilions. The principal advantage of Pavilion architecture is the ease with which units can be renovated without disturbance to neighboring wards and the rapidity with which further units can be added. This design allowed the hospital to be divided into geographic areas serving particular medical disciplines. However, these same factors implied several disadvantages. They made for a disjointed, sprawling hospital where wards, theaters, and administration buildings were scattered and often linked only by open-air pathways.

Early in 1946, negotiations for the transfer of Baragwanath to the Transvaal Provincial Administration (TPA) began. Although the long-term use of the hospital had been a consideration right from its planning stages, debates about the actual suitability of the hospital for use as a general hospital now surfaced. Some argued that because the hospital was built as a war emergency hospital designed for speed of completion and not for economy of function, it would not be well-suited to function as a general hospital. Medical officials complained that the hospital lacked a casualty or outpatient department, had an outdated heating system, and that the staff housing, consisting of merely a military camp, would be costly to deal with.[16] The TPA however, had little choice. The need for a hospital to serve the ever-expanding African population in the area and the cost savings inherent in making use of the existing structure superseded any concerns about the suitability of the premises. This was, after all, a hospital to serve African patients during an increasingly segregationist era and thus patient comfort or, indeed, suitability were not a central concern of the administration. First, the site was not quite as accessible as originally thought. There had been talk of the possibility of extending the railway and placing a station at the entrance to Orlando, which would be nearer to the hospital than the station at Nancefield, about 3¾ miles away.[17] This, however, never came about, and access to the hospital was a continual problem. Until the 1970s there was no bridge across the main road in front of the hospital, forcing patients to run the gauntlet of heavy traffic merely to enter the hospital. When the hospital opened as a civilian hospital it was still, and is today, a maze of single blocks and open-air passages over 100 acres of land. Indeed, it was said that for years it was impossible to get from the emergency room to the operating theaters without being wheeled by a porter down an open corridor. Despite building plans being drawn up and presented to the state in 1949 and again in 1953, the hospital staff faced a ream of justifications for why the state would not provide funding for upgrades. For example, it was argued that "open corridors with the single-story wards may be old-fashioned but they probably keep the rate of cross-infection down."[18] Later, increasingly racist rhetoric was used to justify lack of action. Dr. D. Kritzinger, deputy director (inspections) of the TPA, was reported to have made the explosive statement that "the population of Soweto consisted of Third World people who slept on the floor at home and didn't need beds in hospital. It was official policy not to improve facilities at 'Bara' until blacks contributed more to the economy."[19] Similar thinking led to the argument that prefabricated additions were a preferable form of expansion as opposed to building double-story wards because, the administration argued, "African tradition dictates that they don't feel comfortable on the upper-stories of multiple level wards."[20]

From 1948 there was an additional role-player in the redesign of the hospital: the University of the Witwatersrand (Wits). Wits was committed to using Baragwanath to train both black and white medical students, and the hospital would, over the ensuing years, become one of the university's largest teaching centers. In some cases rooms were converted for teaching purposes—for example, the convalescent Officers' Dining Room was converted into the large lecture theater—while others were built from scratch.[21] The level of modification needed to convert the hospital varied substantially between departments. Some aspects of the hospital needed little modification at all. Professor of surgery William Underwood, in a letter to Dr. W. Waks, the acting medical superintendent of Johannesburg, suggested that, "the operating theatre is suitable in every way and will be quite adequate for the work. It is taken that the theatre equipment be included in the 'take over,' this is important."[22]

New buildings that were constructed right away included residential accommodation for about 120 black students and ten white students. The Hospital Board, with provincial administration agreement, allocated a site on the southern boundary (some distance from the wards) to the university to erect a hostel.[23] Once completed, the hostel, common rooms, and lavatories were all segregated.[24] Doctors' eating, sleeping, and tea facilities were segregated. Black doctors and students were made to use prefabricated buildings that compared unfavorably to the facilities allocated to whites.[25] Even the rationale behind some of the building expansion at the hospital was fundamentally rooted in apartheid logic. For example, the establishment of a maternity ward at Baragwanath in the late 1960s had as much to do with the government's desire to prevent black women from giving birth at the Bridgman Memorial Hospital, situated in "white Johannesburg" as it did with the needs of the Soweto population. The state feared that an increasing number of black children born at Bridgman might claim rights under section 10 of the Group Areas Act to remain in Johannesburg.[26] Whatever the reason, the TPA continued to obstruct hospital plans for major developments of the hospital site. Most of the wards, doctors' accommodations, and specialist unit buildings added in the late 1960s and early 1970s were prefabricated temporary buildings placed in the open spaces between the existing wards.

The two exceptions to this were the construction of the double-story operating theaters (still in use today), which was completed in 1969, and the specialized maternity hospital, commissioned and completed in 1973. The hospital administration made much of the fact that the wards in this section of the hospital were designed in such a way as to maximize the warmth and lighting that could be provided by the sun.

By the 1980s the apartheid state was coming under increasing internal and external pressure, and as townships such as Soweto burned, Prime Minister P.W. Botha imposed a state of emergency, which lasted for the rest of the decade and which brought with it increasingly violent state-sponsored oppression. At the same time, limited reforms were introduced that aimed to reinforce white control over politics while adapting certain aspects of apartheid to the changing social and economic conditions.[27] These reforms included an increase in state funding to black hospitals. While this had almost no effect on relieving the major inequalities in South Africa's health service, it provided the state with justification for the myth that it was providing high-quality care to the urban African population. Baragwanath was central to this myth. Not only was it the largest non-military government institution in the township, which had by then become the heart of the anti-apartheid resistance movement, but also it did, in fact, have pillars of excellence. In the context of apartheid South Africa, the provincial authorities and the state stressed the high-quality, highly technical care available at Baragwanath, their "showpiece," to illustrate the kind of services they were providing for the black popula-tion. Thus, the TPA spent more than 23 million rand on Baragwanath during the 1980s. Among the projects undertaken was the building of a new administration block that did nothing to ease the overcrowding. Rather, it further removed the hospital administration from the rest of the institution by insulating it in a multistory building. A number of doctors referred to this building as the administration *laager*. The reference to the Afrikaans word for the mobile fortifications made by the Voortrekkers out of their wagons to protect them from African attacks during their nineteenth-century journeys through the South African interior was pur-poseful and politically astute. Other projects of limited practical benefit were the construction of a new 8 million rand nurses' home and training center, the building of new gateposts, and the installation of new boilers and a telephone exchange.[28]

None of these projects addressed the central concerns of the staff and patients. For these groups the central concern was that patient numbers had reached astronomical levels, with wards running at 120 percent bed occupancy in the late 1980s. The simmering issue of persistent overcrowding, underfunding, and drastic understaffing was thrust into the public domain by a letter of protest signed by 101 Baragwanath doctors. The original letter, which derided the deplorable conditions at the hospital, was printed in the *South African Medical Journal* in September 1987. The letter highlighted that despite the increased spending at the hospital, little was actually being done to ease congestion or improve the horrendous conditions that were fundamentally rooted in the apartheid system. The circumstances surrounding the writing of the letter and the subsequent fallout did, in fact, bring some material benefit to the hospital. Wits University appealed to the private sector for a donation of 4 million rand to extend each of the thirteen medical wards by two beds and to erect prefabricated structures to accommodate the overflow.[29] This was done with the support of the Soweto community and the Transvaal administrator, Danie Hough. While the TPA had not undertaken any such initiatives themselves, they seemed happy to support those of the university and to take advantage of the opportunities this created, not only to ease the overcrowding in the wards but also to provide some positive publicity.[30] In November 1989 the twelve ward extensions built with the money generously donated by private enterprise were opened.

In 1990 government hospitals were desegregated and this brought Baragwanath to the brink of the New South Africa. After the 1994 democratic election, the hospital at last began to serve a democratic South Africa where the South African Bill of Rights states that "everyone has the right to have access to health care services."[31] This transformation can best be seen in the renaming of the hospital as Chris Hani Baragwanath, after the slain African National Congress leader and *Umkhonto we Sizwe* (MK) activist.

Notes

1. L. Spies, "The History and Establishment of Baragwanath Hospital: A Comprehensive Overview of the Establishment of the Hospital and Its History up to 1980" (unpublished paper, 1980), Bara PR Archives, History File 1.
2. H.J. Martin and Neil Orpen, *South Africa at War, Military and Industrial Organization and Operations in Connection with the Conduct of the War, 1939–1945* (Cape Town: Purnell, 1979), 96; W. Otto,

Chief of the SADF, to Mr. L. Spies, "History of the 130 Imperial Military Hospital, Baragwanath, 1941–1947," March 20, 1977, 1-2, Bara PR Archives. There is a surprising paucity of secondary sources on Allied medicine during the Second World War. One significant exception is M. Harrison, *Medicine and Victory, British Military Medicine in the Second World War* (Oxford: Oxford University Press, 2004). However, this work tends to focus on medicine on

Baragwanath Hospital Buildings

the front rather than in hospitals in the Empire such as Baragwanath.

3. WHSL, "Evidence of the National Health Service Commission," Evidence of Col. K.F.T. Mills, Director of Hospitals under DGMS 2 (December 10, 1942), 2,079.

4. Ibid, 2,079; C. van den Heever, "Baragwanath Hospital—the Beginning," *Adler Museum Bulletin*, 19:1 (March 1993), 10.

5. "Special Report by the Medical Officer of Health (G.D. Laing) to the Public Health Committee on Medical and Hospital Services for Non-Europeans," January 7, 1941, SAB, GES 2891, PH22, Newspaper articles included: "Unions Health Provisions Neglected," *Rand Daily Mail*, May 6, 1940; "Dean Condemns Conditions at Native Hospital," *Rand Daily Mail*, March 9, 1942; "Belated Action," *Rand Daily Mail*, March 11, 1942. These articles were certainly noticed by the National Government: Chief of the News Section for Director of Information to Minister of Public Health, "Native Hospitalisation," February 28, 1942, SAB, GES 1205, 230:23. Private letters include SAB, NTS 2920, 356:303, Mrs C.E. Moore to Minister of Native Affairs (Denys Reitz) regarding the establishment of hospital buildings at Orlando Township, April 3, 1941. Secondary works that expand on this point include: Jeeves, "Public Health," 79–102; S. Marks and N. Andersson, "Industrialisation, Rural Health and the 1944 National Health Services Commission in South Africa," in S. Feierman and J. Janzen (eds.), The Social Basis of Health and Healing in Africa (Berkeley: University of California Press, 1992), 131–61; D. Yach and S. Tollman, "Public Health Initiatives in South Africa in the 1940s and 1950s," *American Journal of Public Health*, 83 (1993), 1,043–50.

6. Important recent work on this topic includes: Shula Marks, "South Africa's Early Experiment in Social Medicine: Its Pioneers and Politics," *American Journal of Public Health* 87 (1997), 452–9; Alan Jeeves, "Public Health in the Era of South Africa's Syphilis Epidemic of the 1930s and 1940s," *South African Historical Journal*, 45 (2001), 79–102; Howard Phillips, "The Grassy Park Health Centre: A Peri-Urban Pholela?" in Saul Dubow and Alan Jeeves (eds.), *South Africa's 1940s: Worlds of Possibilities* (Cape Town: ABC Press, 2005), 108–29.

7. Provincial Secretary H. Pentz to Superintendent of Johannesburg Hospital, K. Mills, "Non-European Hospital Services: Johannesburg," September 12, 1941, SAB, JHM 116, 615, 49–51.

8. Minute from Department of Public Works, "Proposed Hospital in the Orlando Area of Johannesburg," January 11, 1941, SAB, PWD 1064, 8:2547; W. Otto, Chief of the SADF, to L. Spies, "History of the 130 Imperial Military Hospital, Baragwanath, 1941–1947," March 20, 1977, 1–2, Bara PR Archive.

9. Gwen Ramokgopa, Gauteng Health MEC, "Address on the visit of Italian President Carlo Ciampi to Chris Hani Baragwanath Hospital," March 15, 2002, http://www.gpg.gov.za/docs/sp/2002/sp0315a.html.

10. SAB, PWD 1064, 8 (2547), Holdgate (District Representative, Public Works) to Lt. Col. Norburn, "Proposed Hospital in the Orlando Area of Johannesburg," February 6, 1941, 2.

11. SAB, GES 1440, 466 (19), Letter from Director General of Medical Services to the Secretary of Defense, "Site for Imperial Hospital: Johannesburg," April 24, 1941.

12. SAB, PWD 1064, 13:2547 Red Cross—St. John National Coordinating Committee to Secretary of Defense, June 24, 1946; SAB, PWD 1064, 13 (2547), Letter from P.B. Smuts, Secretary for Defense to Secretary for Public Works, April 18, 1947.

13. SAB, PWD 1064, 8:2547, Holdgate (District Representative, Public Works) to Lt. Col. Norburn, "Proposed Hospital in the Orlando Area of Johannesburg," February 6, 1941, 3.

14. L. Spies, "The History and Establishment of Baragwanath Hospital: A Comprehensive Overview of the Establishment of the Hospital and Its History up to 1980"; "Johannesburg, Baragwanath Military Hospital Contracts" (1941), SAB, PWD 1064, 5:2547.

15. J. Taylor, *The Architect and the Pavilion Hospital: Dialogue and Design Creativity in England 1859–1914* (London: Leicester University Press 1997), vii.

16. Provincial Administrator to Secretary of Public Health, "Baragwanath Military Hospital," August 6, 1947, SAB, GES 1598, 6 (623), 11; Secretary to the Treasury from Provincial Secretary, "Baragwanath and Tara Hospitals," April 8, 1948, SAB, GES 1598, 6 (623), 11.

17. Memorandum to the Secretary of Health (G.W. Gale) from the Under Secretary (H. Pentz), "Baragwanath Military Hospital," February 13, 1947, SAB, GES 1440, 466 (19), 5.

18. A. Dubb, "Baragwanath Hospital 1948–1972: The Department of Medicine: The First 25 Years," *Adler Museum Bulletin*, 24 (1) (July 1998), 3–5.

19. Ibid; "Bara Dossier of Shame," *Sunday Times*, October 2, 1988. See also DMF, Schamroth Memorandum, February 24, 1987, which records a conversation between Kritzinger, Schamroth, Blumsohn and Krut in which Kritzinger expressed similar sentiments.

20. Chris van den Heever, January 24, 2003.

21. Ibid.

22. W.E. Underwood to W. Waks, May 9, 1947, SAB, JHM 118, 625, 46–47.

23. Letter from Mr I. Glyn Thomas, Registrar, University of the Witwatersrand, to Dr. Waks, Acting Superintendent, Johannesburg Hospital, Johannesburg, May 27, 1947, SAB, JHM 118, 625, 46–47.

24. Ibid.

25. See, for example: Haroon Saloojee, Annexure B: Written Testimony Submitted to the IRC of the Faculty of Heath Sciences, Professor Y. Veriava, August 31, 2004, 92, WHSR, M 3 (40), IRC.
26. Chris van den Heever, January 24, 2003; B. Lawson, "The Development of the Maternity Ward at Baragwanath" (unpublished paper, June 1980), vdH Papers. On the Bridgman Memorial Hospital, see: R.A. Shiels, "The Bridgman Family in Medical and Missionary Work in Southern Africa, 1860–1946," *Africana Notes and News*, 28:4 (December 1988); Catherine Eileen Burns, "Reproductive Labors: The Politics of Women's Health in South Africa, 1900–1960" (Northwestern University Ph.D. thesis, 1995).
27. Nigel Worden, *The Making of Modern South Africa: Conquest, Segregation and Apartheid* (Oxford: Blackwell, 1994), 121; William Beinart, *Twentieth Century South Africa*, 247–8; Craig Charney, "Class Conflict and the National Party Split," *Journal of Southern African Studies*, 10 (1984), 269–82.
28. *Administrator, Transvaal, and Others v. Traub and Others* 1989 (4) SA 731 (A), Affidavit, H. Van Wyk, 112–13; H. van Wyk, Director of Hospital Services, TPA, "Conditions at Baragwanath," *South African Medical Journal*, 72 (November 1987), 791; P. Kramer, "Bara One of the Best, Says Hospital Service Chief," *Sunday Express*, March 10, 1985.
29. Clive Rosendorff, Dean of the Wits Faculty of Medicine, "Press Statement," January 18, 1989, Wits Archives, Bara. B2.4 (7). See also media reports, such as: T. Younghusband, "We're Going to Help Bara, Says Wits," the *Star*, January 26, 1989, and P. Devereaux, "Shot in Arm for Crowded Bara," *Saturday Star*, March 4, 1989.
30. See, for example, T. Younghusband, "Bara's Patients get Beds," the *Star*, September 29, 1989, which contains a photograph of Transvaal MEC for Hospital Services, Mr. Daan Kirstein, standing smiling next to a patient in a new ward.
31. Constitution of the Republic of South Africa Act No. 108 of 1996, Chapter 2, Article 27(a).

Baragwanath Hospital Buildings

Inspired Hope from an Icon of Decay

Jay Siebenmorgen

Jay Siebenmorgen, AIA, LEED AP, is the design principal of NBBJ Architects'
New York office; he is also currently an adjunct assistant professor of architecture at Columbia University.

According to a report published by the United Nations in June 2013, the current world population of 7.2 billion is projected to increase by a billion over the next twelve years and reach 9.6 billion by 2050. Most of this growth will occur in developing countries, with more than half in Africa. By 2030, 5 billion people will live in cities. These figures, combined with an increase in life expectancy, point to urgent challenges in increased urban density.

The aspiration of all cities is to develop a framework to promote a healthy, happy, and fulfilling lifestyle. Consequently, the topic of urban health is at the center of discussion on city growth today. Many developed cities around the world are implementing smart growth programs focused on the design of streets and buildings to promote healthier lifestyles, fostering new potentials for human experience while fighting epidemics such as obesity and type 2 diabetes. The release of New York City's Active Design Guidelines in 2010, a manual of strategies for healthier buildings and urban landscapes, is one such example.

The issues of developed cities seem minor when compared with those of developing countries. In developing countries, we see cities with indeterminate paths and urban footprints that read more as urban chaos than focused planning for urban health. But there are also cities that were once very strategic, yet in spite of their efforts and successfully built environments, a history of poor political mandates dismantled their urban fabric, leaving in their wake cities of decay. Where the framework and built foundations of a city have existed for decades, architecture may become the catalyst for change.

In the spring of 2013 I had the privilege to co-lead a graduate studio at Columbia University, with the agenda of researching the intersections between urban health and architecture. To uncover legible contrasts, we decided to visit two cities with different backgrounds: Copenhagen and Johannesburg. We studied Copenhagen as the exemplar of a vibrant city with a planning process that has resulted in great infrastructure and a very agreeable lifestyle. In contrast, Johannesburg reached notoriety for apartheid and the resulting urban decay through the 1990s. But it is a city on the rebound.

In the middle of the last century, Johannesburg was viewed as a progressive city instituting model urban planning. As with many cities around the world, Johannesburg experienced significant growth and urban development with the end of World War II. The 1970s saw a flourish of construction activity and an increase in density in the central business district, while investments also occurred in experimental privatized communities in the suburbs. The story reads similar to many cities in the United States after World War II: highways were built, suburban sprawl ensued, and, as a result, the inner-city core became challenged, breeding urban decay. In 1973, Standton City opened in a suburb northeast of downtown Johannesburg. Standton City housed a large shopping mall and office spaces, and eventually became the generator for a larger self-contained, suburban-gated community. The development was a great success, encouraging similar developments to follow and further increasing the hold of apartheid on the city.

But downtown communities did not give up. Adjacent to and northeast of the Central Business District is a dense vertical residential neighborhood called Hillbrow. Although originally designated a "whites only" area in the 1970s under apartheid, Hillbrow reached a vibrant density that fostered an ethnic "gray zone," and eventually it became the first identifiably progressive gay and lesbian neighborhood in South Africa. Such diversity created a community and lifestyle that was often compared to living in Greenwich Village in New York City. The allure was so strong, the population increased to a density unsustainable by the neighborhood infrastructure, resulting in increased crime rates and a middle-class exodus

Inspired Hope from an Icon of Decay

to the suburbs. With the continued investment in suburban developments, urban decline began to occur in the 1980s, and by the '90s Hillbrow was the urban slum that persists to the present day.

The heart of Hillbrow is Pretoria Street, the main commercial avenue. Walking down it today, it is easy to see how this thriving community occurred. The buildings are a melting pot of modernism, where you see pervasive influences from Le Corbusier to the corduroy concrete of Paul Rudolph. There are beautiful Art Deco buildings next to buildings with stripped-down motifs akin to Adolf Loos. In its prime, Hillbrow was no doubt the place to be. Today, however, the buildings are in a state of depression. The street fronts are cluttered and the towers are riddled with broken glass and missing windows across their facades. But there is a visible, thriving population and economy where the experience is captivating and troubling at the same time. The irony in this fabric of decayed buildings is the ubiquitous surface textures of satellite dishes everywhere—a clear sign of flourishing occupancy. The streets are lined with myriad commercial storefronts, street vendors, farmers markets, small "muti" markets selling traditional medicines, and an abundance of people working and loitering.

Hillbrow is clearly a stressed and rough neighborhood, but in its condition of poverty there is energy and vibrancy that is stimulating. It is a transitory neighborhood with a complex cultural climate that has a beauty to it, yet the living conditions are dirty and alarming. As architects we're taught to solve problems—especially if an urban condition is regarded as a "slum," it must be fixed. But how do you remedy decay without removing Hillbrow's vibrancy? Gentrification would appear inevitable, and there are already signs of it occurring. Looking beyond Pretoria Street there is one building in Hillbrow that reads as a case study in how the neighborhood is counter-acting the past thirty years and acting as a catalyst for change: Ponte City.

Ponte City is the most prominent of all Hillbrow high-rises. It is a tower that slips beyond the hold of the Hillbrow grid, even of the city itself. Perched on the edge of a ridge, its vertical impact is amplified, giving it a prominence and presence in the urban terrain and making a strong first

Siebenmorgen

impression as you approach the city from the airport. The ridge is called the Witwatersrand (White Water's Ridge), so-named for marking the watershed between north and south Johannesburg. The Central Business District is to the southwest below the ridge, with the Hillbrow district located on the north. Ponte City is a few blocks southeast of Pretoria Street, where the commercial storefronts disappear and the neighborhood is more specifically residential.

Ponte City is a development with a complex history. Designed by architects Mannie Feldman, Mandred Hermer, and Rodney Grosskopf, the tower's completion and occupation in the 1970s represented the pinnacle of class segregation, where the tower gained prominence in the city as a residential place of opulence. In reality, Ponte City was not much different in program when compared to the gated communities being built in the suburbs: it was essentially a high-rise gated community in downtown with all the required amenities for living, including retail stores, a concert venue, tennis court, swimming pool, and bowling alley. Its status as the tallest residential tower in South Africa, combined with a whites-only designation, further elevated Ponte City as a place of prestige.

With the demise of downtown and Hillbrow in the 1980s, Ponte's reputation declined from an "icon of decadence" to an "icon of decay," where intense crime and drug use occurred. The building became half-vacant as a result of white flight to the suburbs, causing property owners to drop rents drastically and cut building services to maintain cash flow. Ponte City continued to operate at a loss and further spiraled into a state of decay. Gaining access to the tower was difficult, further amplifying the urban legend.

The tower is a cylinder, austere with a clarity and vertical scale that sets it apart from the surrounding neighborhood and the density of the central business district to the west. A cylindrical form is not necessarily unique when compared to modern towers, but in 1975 it was the first cylindrical skyscraper to be built in South Africa. The base is predominantly cast-in-place concrete combined with pre-cast concrete corduroy elements, which categorize Ponte as a Brutalist building. The pre-cast

Inspired Hope from an Icon of Decay

PONTE CITY FROM THE STREET
(GOOGLE 2013 CDNGI DIGITALGLOBE)

Siebenmorgen

continues into the tower, where it becomes an equal proportional layering of glass and concrete, up fifty-four stories, capped off with a four-story, steel-structured billboard—the largest in South Africa and fully illuminated at night.

When studying the tower in the plan, it becomes evident how much the site influenced the design. Hillbrow's grid stops at the south edge of the ridge due to the extreme slope, as evidenced by sparse building in this zone. The builders of Ponte clearly saw the potential to do something different in the city on such a challenging site. In the plan, the building appears like nothing else in the city, almost alien in nature. The circular plan has appendages spiraling off to respond to site function. The tower's main connection to the Hillbrow neighborhood is via a bending, sloped drive to the north. To the south a spiraling ramp descends the slope to access the parking garage. Wrapping the tower at the base is a deep floor plate where the original amenities and retail galleries activated the pedestrian level. The base peels open toward the west to create a large forecourt plaza.

What an outside observer does not see is the large, open internal core, approximately 30 meters in diameter, that forms the main organizing parti of the entire development. The open core is a place where people are said to have leaped to their death intentionally, and where others fell to their death accidentally. At one point, trash was piled four stories high when occupants used the core as a dumping ground.

At the time Ponte City was designed, the developer wanted to maximize the number of units, which resulted in the tall height of fifty-four floors. A city bylaw at the time required all kitchens and bathrooms to have a window. This rule, combined with tight site constraints, drove the architects to design a single-loaded, circular plan, wrapping the large open-air core that would allow natural light to enter on both sides of the units. The circulation and residential units together measure approximately 10 meters in depth to the exterior face. Within the circular plan, the residential program is layered with the circulation corridor along the interior core, then the support spaces of kitchens and bathrooms,

89

AERIAL VIEW OF TOWER (GOOGLE 2013 CDNGI DIGITALGLOBE)

followed by the bedrooms and living rooms on the perimeter with amazing city views.

What is notable is that the tower seems to turn its back on Hillbrow. The elevator core is placed on the northwest face so no apartments have views in that direction. It feels as though the building is not committed to any neighborhood, that it somehow stands apart even from the larger world of Johannesburg. And yet, despite—perhaps even because of—its willful distancing from Hillbrow and Johannesburg at large, Ponte City offers a unique setting to investigate how the power of existing architecture, when rediscovered, may set in motion a positive influence on surrounding neighborhoods.

We visited the tower in the spring of 2013. With the help of our local driver, we gained access to the building management office, where, after a tense conversation, the managers allowed us with our students into the building, assisted by one of their staff. It was evident from our conversation that many try to get into the building on a regular basis, especially groups interested in doing research. Once past the main office, you are led to a security center where access is restricted by finger-scanning technology and full-height security turnstiles. This caused the group a moment of pause as we experienced Ponte City's intentions of changing for the better, but with clear restrictions imposed on its relationship to the outside world.

The entrance plaza and interior commercial alley was mostly open, recently renovated with a small café and sparsely furnished computer center, with many other spaces appearing to await new use. Entering by the elevators, the drama of the tower unfolds. You cannot resist moving immediately to the open center core. The power of the space is undeniable, transporting you into another world. It is shockingly quiet and still, with no activity. Looking up, the glare of the open oculus blurs a reading of where the tower actually ends, distorting your perception of scale as you read an endless, serene grid disintegrating into ethereal light. Looking down, you view the fully exposed rock of the ridge six stories below, as natural light filters through the open-air base parking structure. With no landscaping or evident attempt to hone down the rock, you experience the raw condition of how the tower is built into the side of the ridge. Experiencing the open core, one can read dual symbolic parallels: the first, apartheid, with its defined purpose of segregation echoed in Ponte City's core of introverted containment; the second, the city of Johannesburg and its people, aspiring toward wellness and a brighter future and quality of life, looking to the light above.

The core is predominantly defined by the repetition of the residential grid. While it is horizontally banded, the core has a vertical rhythm and pace that is mitigated by taller floors at the base, which slow one's reading of the tower as it engages the earth. In this moment, the base program appears as unique design elements that offset monotony. Retail spaces are expressed through a series of concrete cupped balconies extruding out into the core. A pair of stairs take on different personalities—one a grand, three-story, formed concrete structure powerfully composed as an accordion X-brace; the other more rudimentary, clad in vertical wood panels, spanning the vertical stretch of the core with its tall, slender line contrasting the stacked horizontal grid. Compositionally, the interdependency of each element balances the space.

Inspired Hope from an Icon of Decay

INTERIOR VIEW OF TOWER (GOOGLE 2013 CDNGI DIGITALGLOBE)

Standing in this space revealed sectional properties of the tower that appear to benefit the performance of the building. The open-air parking garage stacked under the cylindrical tower permits air to flow through, up and out of the core, offering passive cooling effects for all of the units, as well as maintaining ventilation for any unsanitary smells. The shallow floor plate, combined with positive and negative air pressure, would suggest that wind easily pulls through the slender depth of the apartment units, an ideal passive design strategy for the climate Johannesburg enjoys.

We took the elevator up to the last stop and then walked up several flights to level fifty-four, the highest floor, to view a newly renovated suite. Walking along the interior circulation corridor you suddenly become aware of the fragile state of the glazing system. The single-pane glass grid spans floor-to-floor and is constructed of thin steel framing with operable windows. It effectively maximizes natural light and ventilation, but in its state

Siebenmorgen

INTERIOR VIEW OF TOWER (GOOGLE 2013 CDNGI DIGITALGLOBE)

of disrepair, thin structure, and randomly broken and missing window-panes, it leaves you with a very low sense of physical security. It is easy to understand how someone could fall from any level.

The new units are understated with clean, durable materials—ebonized wood doors, ceramic tile flooring, and new modern kitchens. The finishing touches are white crown moldings and pendant light fixtures you might find in most suburban homes. Opulence has returned! This is the most confused moment in the experience of Ponte City. A tower with such powerful architectural composition is suddenly compromised with trivial decoration, as though creature comforts and homogenous finishes could transport tenants to a world beyond the weight of Johannesburg. Surely the renovated units could have been designed with an aesthetic more in tune with the architecture, more expressive of their time and a city being reborn.

Inspired Hope from an Icon of Decay

INTERIOR VIEW OF TOWER (GOOGLE 2013 CDNGI DIGITALGLOBE)

These apparent contradictions are mitigated when you realize the views out to the city are extraordinary. The brilliance of the tower's siting and design becomes clearly evident. This is a special place in the context of Johannesburg. With the siting of the tower on the ridge above the city and with no neighboring towers, it's hard to imagine any of the units having a bad view. Suspended in space above Johannesburg, the interior of these new units seems to exist in another world when considered in the context of the architectural whole of Ponte Tower, let alone the neighborhood of Hillbrow.

Exiting the apartment exposes a palpable tension. As you turn and look back, through the entrance door to the rugged architecture of the interior core, you receive a sensory reality check of where you are and what you are experiencing. In this place of dual identities, you are standing in the heart of this "icon of decay" while experiencing the irony of an optimism exhibited in a freshly renovated suburban unit, all only a few blocks away from the seedy existence of Pretoria Street. It is a reflective strategy on how to refresh the architectural core of Hillbrow, by bringing back architectural vibrancy via the foundation of existing infrastructure. It makes it easy to believe in the future of not only the tower but of greater Hillbrow as well.

Taking the elevator down to the base of the parking structure, we walked out onto the jagged rock slope upon which the tower rests. It feels like an alien world, fully illuminated by the natural light bouncing in from the parking garage and filtering down from the oculus above. It is a space of unsettling power that leaves you no choice but to look up. It is difficult to ease thoughts, or dreams, of everything that occurred here, as well as the immense possibilities for its future; a place with such a strong gesture toward intimacy and introvert containment, yet porous and open ended. This tension is what creates powerful architecture.

Our tour complete, we worked our way up the spiraling car ramp on the south side of the tower to the entrance plaza. Exiting the complex there is a sense of optimism. Granted, there is a long way to go for a full rehabilitation of the tower, but the unique properties of this building lay the

Inspired Hope from an Icon of Decay

groundwork for a future latent with possibilities. Perhaps Ponte Tower's separation from the city grid is what has enabled its apparent rebound today. Perhaps its seclusion on the edge of the neighborhood makes it desirable as a destination, a place to be safe and removed from the dangers of the surrounding areas. And perhaps this is a first step in a reverberation and shockwave of positive influence toward Hillbrow's resurgence. Researching the past five years of Ponte City's development, we saw a slow movement toward renewal. One can question the interior material approach and the aesthetic of the finishes, but you cannot question the owners' and residents' evident determination to create a comfortable living experience, and their optimism for Johannesburg's future.

As a tenant living in Ponte City stated reverentially in Philip Bloom's 2012 documentary, with reference to the tower, "I can't see myself leaving. I mean, where do you go after this?" Perhaps now the tower becomes known as an icon of possibility and rejuvenation, a place to live well again in Johannesburg, a place for positive urban health and a catalyst for change.

Bibliography

United Nations Department of Economic and Social Affairs. "World Population Prospects, the 2012 Revision." United Nations: New York. June 17, 2013. http://www.un.org/en/development/desa/publications/world-population-prospects-the-2012-revision.html

Irene Cheng, ed. *Active Design Guidelines, Promoting Physical Activity and Health in Design*. New York City Department of Design and Construction: New York, 2009. http://www.nyc.gov/html/ddc/html/design/active_design.shtml

Hartford, Anna. "Ponte City." *n+1* magazine, June 14, 2013. http://nplusonemag.com/ponte-city.

Ponte Tower. Dir. Philip Bloom. 2012. http://vimeo.com/51295174

Hanes, Stephanie. "Ponte City—a South African Landmark—Rises Again." The *Christian Science Monitor*, February 12, 2008. http://www.csmonitor.com/World/Africa/2008/0212/p20s01-woaf.html

The Council on Tall Buildings and Urban Habitat. The Skyscraper Center (online database). November 26, 2013. http://skyscrapercenter.com/create.php

Bauer, Nickolaus. "Ponte's fourth coming: An urban icon reborn." *Mail & Guardian: Africa's Best Read*. April 20, 2012. http://mg.co.za/article/2012-04-20-pontes-fourth-coming-an-urban-icon-reborn

Geography of Johannesburg. Easy Expat Ltd., November 27, 2008. http://www.easyexpat.com/en/guides/south-africa/johannesburg/overview/geography.htm

Subotzky, Mikhael. "Ponte City Windows, Televisions, Doors—Three Lightboxes." Mikhael Subotzky Archive. 2004–12. http://www.subotzkystudio.com/ponte-city-text-2/

Taxi Rank No. 2

Thorsten Deckler

Thorsten Deckler is an architect practicing in Johannesburg. He is a founding principal of 26'10 South Architects and has taught and lectured at universities in South Africa and abroad.

Diepsloot is a post-apartheid township on the northern fringes of Johannesburg. It is a socially and economically fragile environment, and home to an estimated 150,000 to 200,000 people. It is also a gateway into Gauteng, the province responsible for generating 40 percent of South Africa's and 10 percent of the continent's Gross Domestic Product. The main taxi rank is one of the settlement's most used entry and exit points, and serves thousands of people on their daily commutes to access work, school, services, and opportunities within the conurbation of 12.3 million people. The upgrade of the rank provides a piece of formal infrastructure that addresses some of the dynamic challenges contained in one of the largest and most complex informal settlements in South Africa.

AERIAL VIEW OF TAXI RANK

Located 35 kilometers north of Johannesburg's city center, Diepsloot was established as a relocation area in 1994, the year of South Africa's first democratic elections. Original inhabitants were resettled here from another informal settlement, and subsequently from Alexandra—one of South Africa's largest and oldest black slums—to make way for the presidentially endorsed Alexandra Renewal Project. In the media Diepsloot is often used to represent the failings of contemporary South Africa. Its stark levels of unemployment, crime, underdeveloped infrastructure, inadequate social facilities, and limited economic opportunities are sadly representative of the slums that house more than 20 percent of South Africa's urban population and in which violent service delivery protests and xenophobic attacks continue to flare up. Seventy-five percent of households live in informal structures at densities reaching 260 dwelling units/hectare and with comparatively little public open space. Yet, despite all of these shortcomings and the negative publicity, Diepsloot's unregulated urban fabric, resourceful use of space, mixed functions, and flexibility present positive spatial and social qualities as well as economic opportunities. The settlement supports high densities and pedestrian traffic that engenders quality of life that arguably surpasses many of the subsidized low-income housing built by the government. For Diepsloot, the challenge lies in how to retrofit the necessary services and infrastructure and to afford its most vulnerable citizens secure forms of tenure.

Project Aims

The upgrading of the taxi rank was commissioned by the Johannesburg Development Agency (JDA), a project management and implementation arm of the City of Johannesburg that has carried out several "catalytic" projects, including major transport interchanges in the Johannesburg inner city and Soweto. The JDA's mandate is to conceive of and build infrastructure as public space that will "normalize" and lend a level of dignity to the daily commutes of a large section of the city's population still affected by the spatial segregation of the apartheid city planning. Our appointment, comprising overall as well as detailed urban development frameworks, was awarded via public tender and financed though the National Treasury's Neighborhood Development Partnership Grant

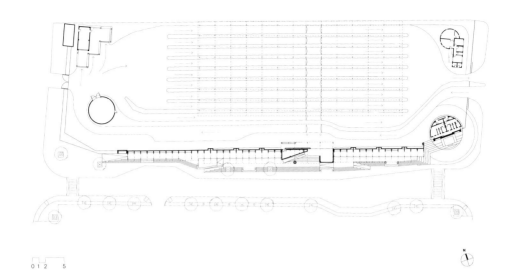

SITE PLAN

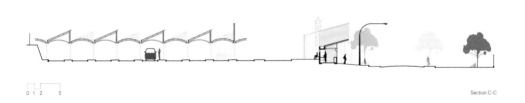

Section C-C

SITE SECTION

99

Taxi Rank No. 2

TRADERS (PHOTOGRAPHS: DAVE SOUTHWOOD)

Taxi Rank No. 2

(NDPG), aimed at facilitating catalytic public infrastructure projects in underserved neighborhoods through public and private investment. The taxi rank presented a "quick win" for the city by ensuring that a large amount of people would benefit from a highly visible investment with economic spin-offs, while higher-level development frameworks were being drafted.

Retrofit

The existing rank functions at capacity from 4:30 a.m. during the work-week, when commutes start early to reach places of employment spread throughout the sprawling metropolis. The original rank comprised the essentials: a roof over part of the queuing aisles, a small office block for the taxi association, some public toilets, and a minimal pedestrian entrance secured by a steel palisade fence. Perhaps cognizant of the larger issues facing the settlement, the original taxi rank was executed in a rudimentary manner and with a minimal sense of civic importance. Tellingly,

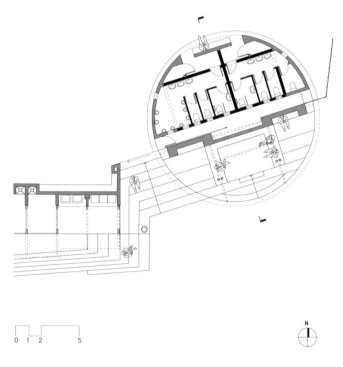

0 1 2   5

N

ABLUTION BLOCK PLAN

the roof over the aisles was built to just accommodate the height of a minibus taxi with the result that the space was so dark that lights had to be left on during the day. Local councilors, traders, various city departments (including road and management agencies), as well as the local taxi association were involved at various stages throughout the design development. The result was an overburdened program, trying to address many needs in a small space. While the utilitarian layout of the rank remains, a set of retrofits now allow it to accommodate a larger amount of users as well as the existing traders operating along the long edge of the rank. The existing administration and ablution block were extended with a reception and boardroom, as well as additional toilets and storerooms. The back of the ablution block was transformed into a sheltered meeting space with views over the settlement. Situated one block from the entrance into Diepsloot it provides a civic space of welcome.

With a high prevalence of crime and vandalism, security is one of the main concerns at the taxi rank. Incorporating public spaces and the existing trader stalls in a linear market and public concourse increases community surveillance. With 2.5-meter-deep lockable stalls and a projecting roof, the market takes the form of a public veranda offering shade and seating opportunities for shopping, eating, and socializing. The concourse incorporates washing-up and refuse collection points as well as open stalls for additional traders. Its western end functions as a bus and informal taxi stop, the latter used during nonpeak hours. Thickening and programming the threshold between street and rank mediates the dichotomy of "inside" and "outside" so common in Johannesburg. In addition, this animated edge reenforces the public nature of the main street. With few formal public spaces in Diepsloot, streets and pavements form the default public realm. Through the provision of lockable shops, and improved amenities for customers, the existing businesses have evolved to include a laundry, cellphone services, household supplies, fruit, vegetables, and baked goods. Food stalls offer a wider range of fare with sit-down lunches regularly served on the concourse. Fireplaces incorporated into the food stalls provide cooking facilities, and decommissioned timber palettes offer cheap sources of fuel. The inclusion of the fireplaces was highly controversial, viewed as backward by the city's management

MAIN PEDESTRIAN ENTRANCE
(PHOTOGRAPH: IWAN BAAN)

INFORMAL ENTRANCE
(PHOTOGRAPH: IWAN BAAN)

agency tasked with taking over the rank once completed. We overcame this resistance, however, by citing the long power outages and relative high costs of pay-as-you-go electricity provided to the stalls. Additionally, we demonstrated that the chimneys could hold billboards—on appropriately engineered concrete bases— that would generate income of $4,000 per month. This finally convinced officials. The advertising is yet to be commissioned, and could subsidize a planned-for photovoltaic installation. We are also developing a system for stall signage and commissioned public art.

Young Cities

Informal settlements such as Diepsloot can be seen as young cities, which have yet to acquire the services, infrastructure, and legal status provided to the formal city. The National Housing Code allows for the creation of new standards when it comes to the upgrading of existing settlements, and the state's developmental rhetoric has shifted from that of "eradication" to "upgrading" (not least due to the formal acknowledgement that the backlog of 2.3 million subsidized houses cannot realistically be met). This is a unique moment in South Africa, in which a potentially viable urban future can be pursued through learning from, and working within, given conditions. There is no point in wishing away divisions of race, class, and income grafted not only into the urban and rural landscapes but also into mind-sets of South Africans. The informal economy, taxi industry, and informal settlements represent, in many ways, appropriate responses evolved to overcome the obstacles of segregation. While their contingent nature and legal conflict with the formal urban system further entrenches difference, their increasing interdependence is a field for intervention in which new rules of engagement are charted. The upgrading of the rank through retrofitting, addition, and adjustment represents, on a small scale, what needs to be undertaken to take apart environments created as an indirect result of apartheid's legacy. While such interventions play an important role in binding places like Diepsloot into the city at large, the informal houses surrounding the rank beg for new forms of development, in which the efforts made by people to construct their own homes is recognized. For architecture, this

MARKET AND PUBLIC PORCH
(PHOTOGRAPH: IWAN BAAN)

may mean engaging with processes of participative decision making in which the role of the architect shifts from expert to that of a socio-technical facilitator skilled in extrapolating spatial scenarios. This will necessitate the crossing of thresholds defining professional disciplines as well as the educational and representative institutions that maintain them. By incrementally bridging informal settlements and the formal city, these largely self-generated environments may play a humanizing role in South African cities.

John Dube, trader:
"It is better since the upgrade. It was dirty on the street.
Now you have your own space, and it is lockable."

Martha & Evelyna, traders:
"It's good, shelter from the rain... I come five o'clock in the morning; I enjoy it...
The customers are more, business is more."

Mariam & Martha, traders:
"It is better... It is safe; we can close and lock, and then go home and not worry."

Lina, trader:
"Before I was selling on the street, without a shelter. Rain was a crisis.
You would run for shelter and leave your stock behind. Now I have shelter; it is secure."

Lidia & Mudzuli, traders:
"The upgrade is good for the community. Before there was nothing, now we have infrastructure.
It is something to be proud of. A legacy for Diepsloot's next generation.
One day we can say to our children: 'I was part of the community that was involved in building it.'"

Jamina, trader:
"Business is going well. Before I was on the street with no shelter.
Now I am indoors and protected from the rain. I can leave my property at the shop and lock it.
There is security at night. I don't have to carry my stock with me every time anymore.
Only when I get new stock."

Kenith, community member and electrician:
"Since the upgrade I enjoy coming here... It is cleaner and the food is better."

Nando, taxi driver and visitor at market:
"I like to come to the market for lunch. Business is good. The food is good."

Daniel, manager and chairman of taxi rank:
"I am happy to use the taxi rank. It's very good. It has become too small; we needed more space...
The taxi rank works well. It has shelter from the rain for the people and the cars.
And it's not windy inside... The office is a good location, near the police station.
We needed more space to accommodate all the taxi owners when having meetings."

Taxi Rank No. 2

To Understand the Rats Is to Know the City[1]

Melinda Silverman

Melinda Silverman is an urban designer and urban policy specialist working with WITS University and UN Habitat. Silverman's research has explored the increasing importance of the urban periphery in the Johannesburg metropolitan system.

Everyone—absolutely everyone—in Johannesburg has stories about rats. Rats haven't exactly been given the freedom of the city; they've taken it— occupying both the neighborhoods of the rich and the neighborhoods of the poor, both the formerly white suburbs and the historically black townships. With a measure of success that continues to elude Johannesburg's human inhabitants nineteen years after the advent of democracy, rats have succeeded in overcoming all the barriers erected by apartheid—spatial buffers, *cordons sanitaire*, race, and class. Rats have become South Africa's truly post-apartheid urbanites. "These rats don't discriminate," says Ronald Springfield, a pest exterminator who has been in the business for thirty-four years. "I get just as many calls from [the luxury suburb of] Sandton as I do from Soweto [the giant black township near Johannesburg]. They are all over greater Johannesburg, in all the suburbs, in slum dwellings and mansions."[2]

Recent research in the city confirms the ubiquity of rats. Koekie Jeremiah, a resident of Kliptown in Soweto is besieged by rats.[3] She will not leave her house at night. She is terrified of the rats that have burrowed under the chemical toilet located in her front yard—in this, one of the oldest black suburbs in Jo'burg that has yet to be connected to waterborne sewerage. A block down the road, Uncle Bolo holds out his hands the width of his chest to show the size of local rats.[4] He says, "There are no longer cats big enough to take on the rats." Herbert Mashishi, a youth activist working out of the Thusong Community Centre in Alexandra, another black township, has stories about rats eating babies, rats attacking the elderly, and even rats gnawing through coffins to dine on dead bodies.[5]

At the opposite end of the socioeconomic spectrum, Sybil Sachs, a longtime resident of up-market Parkview, recalls sitting on her terrace watching the rats swing fearlessly from tree to tree—"like acrobats"—at the bottom of her leafy suburban garden.[6] During the winter months, car repairmen regularly deal with wires and rubber tubes that have been chewed by rats bedding down inside a well-warmed automobile engine.

In the academic literature on health in African cities rats have been receiving pretty good press—which is no press at all.[7] Rats are generally a secretive species, happier under the radar than in the spotlight of the academic microscope. HIV/AIDS has displaced rats as the number-one public health scourge, a spot that they occupied about a century ago.[8] Yet a visit to any part of Johannesburg will reveal something of a renaissance. Today, according to Uncle Bolo, there is a veritable "festival of rats."[9]

Rats are coeval with humans. Wherever humans set up home, rats will follow. Unlike most species, which require highly specialized habitats, rats can live almost anywhere. They are found on every continent on earth (except Antarctica) and can therefore be considered the most successful mammal on the planet along with humans.[10]

Unfortunately, the relationship between rats and humans is exploitatively asymmetrical. Rats have much to gain from coexisting with humans, particularly in cities where water, food, and shelter are guaranteed. Humans have less to gain from rats. Although rats form part of the human diet in some areas of China, and are increasingly being adopted as domestic pets, they are dangerous vectors of disease. The black roof-rat (*Rattus rattus*) is a known bubonic plague carrier; the brown rat (*Rattus norwegicus*) is a carrier of Weil's disease, viral hemorrhagic fever, and hantavirus pulmonary syndrome. Nothing is yet known about the disease-carrying abilities of the mysterious black-and-white rat.[11] These health dangers pose a particular threat in African countries with millions of highly vulnerable, immune-deficient people, with at least 6 million infected with the AIDS virus, of whom 60 percent are also infected with TB and HIV.[12]

To Understand the Rats Is to Know the City

INFORMAL HOMES AND ENCAMPMENTS IN SOWETO
ARE OFTEN BESIEGED BY RATS.
(PHOTOGRAPHS: MELINDA SILVERMAN)

Rats also discourage economic activity. Sibusiso Nyani, a trader at Park Station, the busy intermodal transport exchange in Johannesburg's inner city, which is overrun by rats, says rats are bad for his business, "People don't want to buy from us anymore. When they see the rats they run away."[13] In some areas of Johannesburg, rats have burrowed under the ground so intensively that sidewalks have collapsed.[14]

Cities are an attractive habitat for rats. Both urban decline and, counterintuitively, urban regeneration exacerbate the presence of rats. Foreclosures and abandonment provide rats with comfortable homes. But new construction unearths rats from their burrows.[15] Warmer weather and aging infrastructure also fuel rodent populations.

There are various factors in Johannesburg that make the city particularly conducive to rats. The city's current fluidity, in which informal practices continuously overwrite modernist '60s-style planning, creates new opportunities for rats. In Johannesburg, informal trade, which takes place on sidewalks, is synonymous with rats. This is because the formal waste collection system, which is designed primarily for privately owned plots, cannot adequately deal with the increasing amounts of refuse generated in public space, which is where most informal activity occurs.

Unanticipated land-use changes in the context of urban flux also pose a challenge for Pickitup, the somewhat plaintively named city waste collection utility. Buildings once zoned industrial are now squats used for residential purposes. The police officers who patrol these invaded warehouses carry big sticks, not as a form of protection against potentially antagonistic tenants, but to scare away the rats. In the so-called Ethiopian Quarter, office blocks that once accommodated doctors and dentists have now been converted to shops. Refuse collection systems have not kept pace with these radical changes. In some situations, this failure is probably because of neglect by Pickitup, which has been subject to a series of both scandals and strikes that leave piles of refuse uncollected for many days. But in other instances, it might be a conscious act of withdrawal by the city to displace these unplanned and often illegal land uses.

To Understand the Rats Is to Know the City

The presence of densely packed shacks in many townships also brings rats. The absence of adequate foundations under these flimsy structures allows rats to burrow in and out of people's homes. "It's hard to keep rats out of the shacks," says Herbert Mashishi. "The rats climb in under the zinc and at night they eat from our pots.[16] Alex is a good habitat for rats. The rats work hand in hand with people."[17] Rats tunnel from shack to shack as if on an uninterrupted "freeway."[18]

Many of Johannesburg's residents are disengaged from the reciprocal rights and responsibilities of urban life, either because they are actively angry at the state in the face of unfulfilled hopes or because they aren't particularly invested in the city. "The problem is that people are dumping everywhere and rubble is a very good hiding place. We've tried teaching people not to dump, but they don't care. They hate the council: the community will help the rats as part of their fight against the city. Part of the

A RESIDENT OF ALEXANDRA EXPLAINS THE ISSUE WITH RATS.
(PHOTOGRAPH: MELINDA SILVERMAN)

problem is that for many people in Alex, the place is not home. It's just a place to sleep,"[19] says Mashishi.

City officials acknowledge that rats are a "challenge," municipal spin for what is really a crisis, but they also admit to having no data on the dimension of the problem. The mathematics of rats is that you count the human population and then multiply by factor x. The best hope for most cities is a ratio of 1:1, which would give Jo'burg a population of 3.8 million rats.[20] The worst-case scenario is 1:12, which would bring the figure close to 50 million. The estimate for Paris, for example, is 1:4 and for New York it is 1:10. These numbers suggest a very elastic range. But the math is even more complicated when you factor in the rate at which rats breed: A "dominant male rat may mate with up to twenty female rats in just six hours," says Robert Sullivan, who has written the definitive study on rats in New York.[21] "The gestation period of a pregnant female rat is twenty-one days, the average litter between eight and ten pups. And a female rat can become pregnant immediately after giving birth. If there is a healthy amount of garbage for the rats to eat, then a female rat will produce up to twelve litters of twenty rats each a year. One rat's nest can turn into a rat colony of fifty rats in six months. One pair of rats has the potential of 15,000 descendants in a year.[22]

Notwithstanding an absence of data on rat numbers, the city has come up with various initiatives to reduce rats, particularly in Alexandra—a predominantly black residential area, one of the city's most densely inhabited neighborhoods and a hot spot for rats. "The city of Jo'burg has tried many things to control the rats in Alex," says Mashishi. "They started out with cleanup campaigns, but these didn't work. The campaigns made Alex fresh for half a day, but then it was back to square zero."[23]

"Then the community was crying to the city for poison. But that didn't work either. The people were using the poison on each other. It wasn't safe for babies to have poison lying around. We realized that we were trying to kill the rats, but in the process we were killing the people. There was another campaign with cages. These cages were handed out ward to ward and people were asked to bring their cages in once the rats had

To Understand the Rats Is to Know the City

been caught. The plan was to gas the rats with carbon monoxide, screen for diseases, and then take the dead rats to a disposal site...”[24] But this avenue was not pursued systematically after the National Society for the Prevention of Cruelty to Animals stopped a gassing initiative elsewhere in the city on the grounds of inhumane treatment to rodents.

“After that, the Environmental Health Department for the region introduced an owl box program. This seemed like the most ecologically friendly approach. The schools were targeted as the right place to start the campaign. They put the boxes in schools so that the kids could take care of the owls in the day. Then, when the schools became quiet at night, the owls would start hunting the rats. But this also proved to be a challenge. There are belief systems around here, myths that owls can be used to bewitch people. Their big eyes make them look like people, like spirits. There were *sangomas* (traditional healers) who were killing the owls for *muti* (herbs or animal parts used by healers). Most of the owls were killed.”[25]

Even if the owls hadn’t been slaughtered, it is unlikely that this program would have worked from a numbers perspective. On average, a family of owls can consume 2,500 rats a year, which is hardly enough to dent a rat population that could range from anywhere between 350,000 and about 5 million—the human population of Alex (estimated at between 350,000 and 400,000) multiplied by one or by twelve, depending on the human-to-rat ratio.[26] This might have improved over time if the owls were given the opportunity to breed. Owls can rear up to twenty chicks if food is plentiful.[27] But even so, the rats would have prevailed.

The most controversial campaign to eradicate rats in Alex was launched by a suicide prevention organization called Lifeline. Lifeline had received a donation of hundreds of cellphones by local company 8ta to equip their volunteers, but not all the phones were needed. Lifeline then decided to use the surplus phones to reward Alex residents for every sixty rats caught—dead or alive.[28] However, rumors soon emerged that Alexandra residents had started breeding rats to reach the target.[29]

In the ongoing and unwinnable war against rats it is not hard to believe that rats have supernatural powers. According to Alex resident Leo Ndambini, rats eat used condoms to gain humans' knowledge. "This is why some people think they are maybe so clever."[30] Uncle Bolo also believes other forces might be at work. Aside from the "normal rat...the standard rat, which is gray and will run away when he sees you," there is "a rat which has been sent by witchcraft. This demonic rat—a rat with black in his fur—he will defy you. He doesn't run. When someone wishes poverty on you, these people will send the rats to do the work for them, to take your food. These rats are possessed. They will eat anything. They eat people and they are especially dangerous to small children."[31]

The solution to the rat problem, according to Uncle Bolo is "to get a white rat in the house. Then the other rats—the rats that aren't white—will run away. For rats it's like apartheid all over: *Hier kom die boere.*"[32] Here come the whiteys.

Notes

1. This story owes a debt of gratitude to Dr. Tanya Zack, urban researcher par excellence, a far braver ratter than I, who accompanied me on my rat-seeking expeditions and who facilitated interviews with key informants—Koekie Jeremiah and David Meyers in Kliptown, and Herbert Mashishi in Alexandra. The story is also indebted to Robert Sullivan, whose book on New York, *Rats: Observations on the History and Habitat of the City's Most Unwanted Inhabitants*, brilliantly illustrates how rats can be used as a lens to understand urban conditions.
2. Originally reported on Network 24, www.network24.com.
3. Interview with Koekie Jeremiah, September 17, 2013.
4. Interview with David Meyers, who likes to be called Uncle Bolo, September 17, 2013.
5. Interview with Herbert Mashishi, September 17, 2013. In December 2011, Alexandra resident Nunu Sithole's nine-month-old baby died after being attacked by rats. The rodents had bitten through the baby's diaper and ate away at both her legs. http://ewn.co.za/2013/07/17/Rat-Attacks. Cited August 13, 2013.
6. Interview with Sybil Sachs, September 25, 2013.
7. Michael, Pacione, *Urban Geography: A Global Perspective*, (Oxon: Routledge, 2009).

8. In 1904, parts of Johannesburg were burnt to the ground in a controversial effort to address an outbreak of bubonic plague. Although municipal officials cited rats as the reason for the burning, more recent histories have argued that the destruction of the "Coolie location" was a deliberate attempt to displace residents of Indian origin from the inner city.
9. Interview with David Meyers, September 17, 2013.
10. Dorothy Fragazy and Susan Perry, *The Biology of Traditions: Models and Evidence* (Cambridge, UK: Cambridge University Press, 2003), 165. John McNeil in his masterful *Something New Under the Sun: An Environmental History of the Twentieth Century* (2000) also writes about the successful survival strategies of the rat species, which is famously adaptable and resilient, using catastrophes to increase—rather that reduce—its ecological footprint.
11. Originally reported on Network 24, www.network24.com.
12. Ibid.
13. http://www.news24.com/SouthAfrica/News/Rats-infest-Johannesburg-CBD-20110419. Cited August 13, 2013.
14. http://mg.co.za/article/2012-10-26-00-catch-60-rats-win-a-phone. Cited September 29, 2013.
15. Manhattan experienced a surge in its rat population after the destruction of the Twin Towers,

To Understand the Rats Is to Know the City

which unearthed thousands of rats from their burrows.

16. *Zinc* is township slang for corrugated iron sheeting, the most popular building material in South Africa's informal settlements.

17. Interview with Herbert Mashishi, September 17, 2013.

18. Koekie Jeremiah's phrase for describing the movement of rats in Kliptown.

19. Interview with Herbert Mashishi, September 17, 2013.

20. According to Executive Mayor Mpho Parks Tau's State of the City address (2012), Johannesburg has a population of 3.8 million people. www.Jo'burg. org.za. Cited September 29, 2013.

21. Robert Sullivan, *Rats: Observations on the History and Habitat of the City's Most Unwanted Inhabitants* (New York: Bloomsbury, 2004).

22. Ibid., 9.

23. Interview with Herbert Mashishi, September 17, 2013.

24. Ibid.

25. Interview with Herbert Mashishi, September 17, 2013.

26. United Nations Educational, Scientific, and Cultural Organization, "Presentation of Alexandra Township," http://portal.unesco.org/ci/en/ ev.php-URL_ID=3438&URL_DO=DO_TOPIC&URL_ SECTION=201.html, May 19, 2003.

27. 2 Oceans Vibe, "Johannesburg Chooses Owls to Fight the Rat Plague in Alexandra Township," http://www.2oceansvibe.com/2012/03/15/ johannesburg-chooses-owls-to-fight-rat-plague- inalexandra-township, March 15, 2012.

28. Rudo Mungoshi, "Alex Rat Catchers Rewarded," June 7, 2012, http://www.Jo'burg.org.za/index. php?option=com_content&id=8184:alex-rat- catchers-rewarded&Itemid=266#ixzz2gHwd U6Rz.

29. Interview with an Alex resident who wishes to remain anonymous.

30. Sipho Kings, "Catch 60 Rats–Win a Phone," Mail and Guardian, October 26, 2012, http://mg.co.za/ article/2012-10-26-00-catch-60-rats-win-a-phone.

31. Interview with David Meyers, September 17, 2013.

32. Ibid.

Silverman

Learning from Johannesburg

Mabel O. Wilson

Mabel O. Wilson is the Nancy and George E. Rupp professor at Columbia University's Graduate School of Architecture, Planning and Preservation, where she directs the program for Advanced Architectural Research, co-directs the Global Africa Lab, and is a senior fellow at the Institute for Research in African American Studies in GSAS.

Program. Form. Site. Structure. These were the foundational areas that undergirded U.S. architectural design studio pedagogy in the second half of the twentieth century. The chosen site was typically a local one or an invented context on a bucolic plateau or ideal urban infill. *Program* often defined a civic institution, cultural institution, or private residence. Precedent studies drew from the knowledge learned in foundational architectural history surveys, courses that chronicled a genealogy of Western architectural development. An architect's aesthetic sensibilities and technical expertise formed within this prescribed constellation of references and local contexts. However, with architects now building in many parts of the world, places where they neither work nor live, how should studio—the space for architectural learning where knowledge coalesces—incorporate the global? More specifically, what would an architectural design studio at New York–based Columbia University Graduate School of Architecture, Planning and Preservation (GSAPP) learn from working on projects sited in the South African city of Johannesburg?

Over the past thirty years, the profession and architectural education have embraced new tools of design including parametric modeling and fabrication techniques. But beyond the tools and techniques of practice, the globalization of architecture during that same time span has also cultivated a new set of challenges that reach beyond the remnants of the universal discourse of modernism's international style or the critical regionalism central to postmodernism's contextual bent. These challenges raise questions about how to educate future architects to navigate cross-cultural exchanges; to address problems of climate change around the world; to operate within the contexts of rapid urbanization and its flip side, deindustrialization; and to understand the ways that the rise of neoliberalism has transformed how our shared built realm is stewarded, shifting power from the state authority to the control of private development. More broadly, how can we train architects to recognize how these aforementioned issues concern environmental degradation and have become central to improving the health and well-being of populations around the world? It is imperative that new models of pedagogy and curriculum be tested and launched. Can the global studio be one such pedagogical arena?

To educate an architect in the "arts of building," particularly prior to architecture's professionalization in the nineteenth century, "he"—undoubtedly a gentleman—would have traveled extensively. In Europe and then in the United States, those who wanted to gain expertise in architecture would have been of the aristocracy or emerging elite classes and therefore would have had the time and financial resources to embark upon a Grand Tour of continental Europe. The monuments of antiquity—the Acropolis and the Pantheon—and the great works of the Renaissance—Venice's Piazza San Marco, Palladio's Villa Rotunda, and Bramante's Tempietto along with the landscapes of Switzerland, Italy, and Greece—would be studied in great detail by the gentleman practitioner-in-training. The knowledge gained on these tours would comprise one facet of a broader education on what were then emerging notions of history and culture. These concepts of cultural difference and historical advancement would come to define the uniqueness and superiority of European identity in an age of colonial expansion into the Americas, Asia, and Africa. With the rise of the nation-state and industrialization in the nineteenth century, the need for new types of building for a modern society grew. In response to these needs, the practice of architecture became institutionalized in schools and professional associations. The well-known sites of the Grand Tour—popularized in paintings and prints—became foundational to the histories of Western architecture that were circulated to students of architecture in books and presented to them in lectures on glass slides. Those who could still afford the Grand Tour, such as Le Corbusier in his well-documented *Voyage d'Orient*, for example, continued to make the journey.[1] By the latter half of the twentieth century, the proliferation of

U.S. architecture school–sponsored semester-long study abroad programs in Vicenza, Rome, Florence, Paris, and elsewhere on the European continent, demonstrates how the foundational studies of culture and history are built upon these particular European cultural roots—ones that are presumed to embody transcendent ideals in architecture of truth, beauty, and utility.

If the nineteenth- and twentieth-century education of architects was underpinned by a fundamental European formulation of civilization, then how do we interpret within that body of knowledge encounters with non-European cultures? By the twentieth century, representations of folk, primitive, and vernacular cultures formed the basis for a critique of the ills of industrialization lodged by modernist architects. Modernism achieved this by locating these cultures as lower on the evolutionary scale that propelled modernity ever forward. Architect Adolf Loos stages his dialectic of civilization in his seminal essay "Ornament and Crime" (1908) as follows: "I can tolerate the ornaments of the Kaffir, the Persian, the Slovak peasant woman, my shoemaker's ornaments, for they all have no other way of attaining the high points of their existence." By contrast, civilized men, Loos declares, have progressed because "We [Loos included] have art, which has taken the place of ornament."[2] Fifty years later, architect Aldo Van Eyck's ethnographic interest in the Dogon peoples of Mali made the dialectic of cultural exchange in architecture more apparent. Yet Van Eyck's best intentions relied on the problematic ethnographic methods that maintained African cultural otherness within the spectrum of the primitive. In CIAM's Athens Charter (1933) and Team X's "Doorn Manifesto" (1954), for example, modernism's philosophy of transcendent form and culture defined universal criteria for architecture, a style and set of principles that outlined how to build a new architecture that could be circulated to an international audience and within a postwar world where emerging nations needed architecture to modernize. These universal principles, however, were predicated on long-standing epistemological assumptions about the superiority of particular forms of knowledge, including architecture. Theorist Denise Ferriera da Silva observes in the domination of the modern "project of knowledge" that "throughout the last five centuries or so, Europeans and their descendants have crossed

Learning from Johannesburg

the globe over and over again to appropriate lands, resources and labors."
From these territorial expansions she suggests that "no doubt these
dislocations have instituted the global economic and juridical formations
historical and social scientific literatures apprehend with the concepts of
colonialism, imperialism, modernization, and globalization."[3] Thus, with
its ties to philosophy and history, architectural discourse has always been
implicated in these modern formations. In light of this history, how can
we critically engage the contemporary circulation of architectural knowledge as it moves across global circuits?

The global city has been a term bandied about since the early '90s.[4]
The movement and migration of resources, people, and finished goods
have destabilized modernity's correlation of center and periphery. A
new sphere for architectural production, what Rem Koolhaas called
"Junkspace," requires new approaches. Theorist Okwui Enwezor posits
that the tensions transforming the global city "have produced new
theories and cartographies of space, forms and iconographies of living
and dwelling, strategies of survival, concepts of citizenship, typologies
of difference, demographics of identity and community, and a situational
aesthetics which throw into relief dislocutions in the syntax of the cities'
urban narrative and iconography."[5] How can students and studios fulfill
their educational mandate by working within these new urban spheres of
creation and conflict?

The William Kinne Travel fellowship awards, established in the spirit of
the Grand Tour, have provided funds for students to study architecture in
all parts of the world. In the past few years with the creation of the Kinne
travel studios as a part of the advanced studio sequence, research and
learning through travel have also become a core part of the curriculum.
In 2008, these Kinne travel studios became the basis for the formation of
Studio-X, which operates as an advanced laboratory for the exploration
of cities. With these Studio-X platforms, faculty and students can col-
laborate on long-term studio and research projects in cities like Beijing,
Rio, Mumbai, Istanbul, and Johannesburg with local partners in these cities. Even though students matriculate through the school on a prescribed
sequence of courses, they nevertheless benefit from the long-term

collaborations and cross-pollination of knowledge about architecture and cities. Rather than GSAPP importing expertise in education and research to locations where Studio-X has platforms, the school aims to cultivate "cross-cultural, cross-disciplinary, and cross-continental exchange within and between diverse regions."[6]

A new pedagogical model is emerging that no longer studies architecture as separate from its political, economic, and cultural contexts; in other words, students no longer study architecture within neutral or invented contexts. Instead, pertinent issues such as health and well-being can be examined as part of the building's environment. The studio led by Professor Hilary Sample and architect Jay Siebenmorgen looked closely at how the stress within Johannesburg's urban fabric correlates to the status of public health. These explorations by students—who were from all parts of the globe—included an examination of the significance of the urban infrastructures that link it to transportation, water, and resource networks, along with the sociopolitical structures that shape how and why social inequalities like urban public health become instantiated within sprawling metropolitan regions. These are both the consequence of global forces that shape larger frameworks influencing a population's opportunities and access to resources to improve health, particularly those on an urban scale. Another benefit of traveling to a city like Johannesburg is that students discovered that many of the factors that influence what the studio defined as "urban stress" were specifically local. The studio developed specific typological solutions that drew from local sources and conditions. Admittedly, the available information about Johannesburg and its public health system was fragmentary and a challenge to access. Therefore, the studio pieced together a fuller picture of the city through combing a range of archives, through conversations with experts and locals, and through their own experiences traveling to Copenhagen and Johannesburg. That knowledge was no longer universal and overarching; it required a new productive method of critical engagement compelling students to adapt new perspectives on what they read and saw.

Within the global studio, these local and global relationships necessitate a new set of tools and modes of analysis to decipher what they mean and how to work within them. Today, research in the studio is routine rather than exceptional. In the early '70s Denise Scott Brown and Robert Venturi's studio at Yale University that attempted to create new modes of representation to analyze the sign-based landscapes of the American suburban experience, research compiled in the seminal *Learning From Las Vegas,* suggests that experimentation in pedagogy has always been a key area of architectural education. In light of the outcomes of globalization—urbanization, migration, resource depletion, and climate change—design studios now work outside local contexts in places like Johannesburg and elsewhere around the world. The global studio operates as a critical space where such challenges can be posed and new ideas about architecture can be created and circulated.

Notes

1. Le Corbusier, Guiliano Gresleri, and Fondation Le Corbusier, *Voyage d'Orient: Carnets*, (New York: Phaidon, 2002).
2. Adolf Loos, "Ornament and Crime," in *Programs and Manifestoes on 20th-Century Architecture*, ed. Ulrich Conrads (Cambridge: MIT Press, 1994; org. 1908), 24.
3. Denise Ferreira da Silva, *Toward a Global Idea of Race* (Minneapolis: University of Minnesota Press, 2007), 3.
4. Saskia Sassen, *The Global City*, (Princeton: Princeton University Press, 1991).
5. Okwui Enwezor, "Introduction," in *Under Siege: Four African Cities: Freetown, Johannesburg, Kinshasa, Lagos, Documenta 11 Platform 4.* (Ostfildern-Ruit: Hatje Cantz, 2002), 17.
6. "About Studio-X," http://www.arch.columbia.edu/ studio-x-global/about-studio-x, accessed March 7, 2014.

In urban health, as is the case with urbanism more broadly, global scales inflect the local. Cities and neighborhoods make visible the regional or even worldwide patterns of health that depend on a number of influencing factors. How might we understand the relationship between the city—its infrastructure, development, and demographics—and environmental conditions across continents? How might issues like zoning compound environment to exacerbate or ameliorate the spread of disease, or provoke psychological duress? How might we *see* and quantify urban health?

The following maps attempt just that, through their own particular scales and focuses. Drawing upon spatial analysis of housing, commercial activity, and racialized geography, maps of Johannesburg reveal the economic landscape of apartheid and its correlation to density, mobility, and pollution. They also illustrate the extent to which the South African state has historically conceived of space along racial lines, diagramming, for instance, the precise ethnic compositions of black townships.

Meanwhile, the seductive cartography of thermic sultriness charts regional temperatures across the span of a year. These maps were compiled to understand the spread of epidemic disease during World War Two, and show in vivid relief the climatic conditions that may amplify health crises in overburdened and underserved urban areas. This collection is also an exercise in how to read a map, how to see spatial information relationally, and how to infer correlations between the many scales at which health operates.

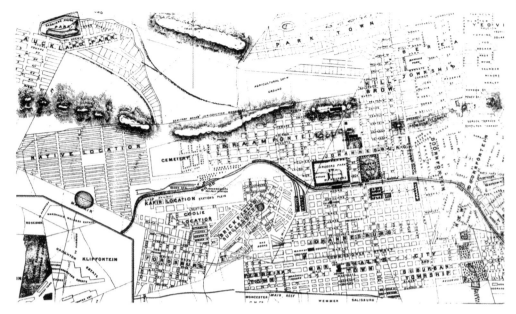

PART PLAN OF JOHANNESBURG 1897

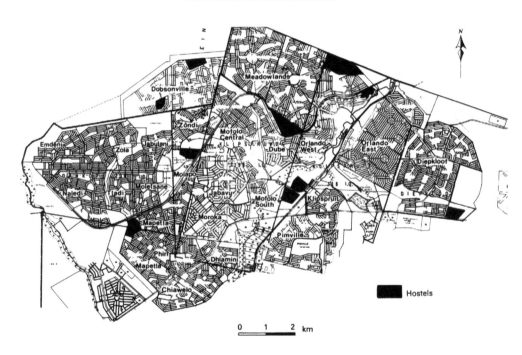

LAYOUT OF SOWETO SHOWING TOWNSHIPS AND HOSTELS, 1980
(SOURCE: MORRIS, PAULINE. *A HISTORY OF BLACK HOUSING IN SOUTH
AFRICA*. JOHANNESBURG: SOUTH AFRICA FOUNDATION, 1981.)

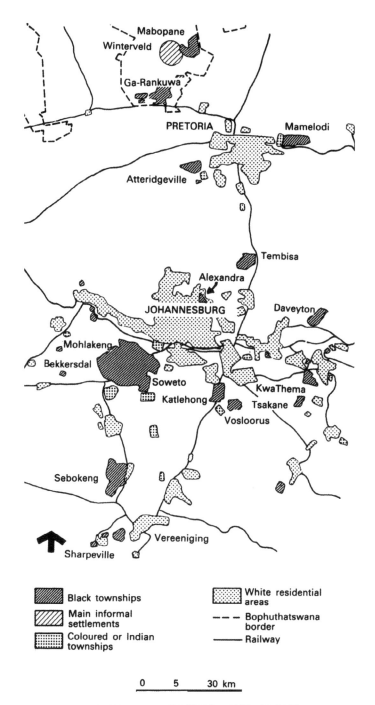

Black townships

Main informal settlements

Coloured or Indian townships

White residential areas

-- -- Bophuthatswana border

—— Railway

0   5   30 km

THE PRETORIA - WITWATERSRAND - VEREENIGING AREA
(SOURCE: MORRIS, PAULINE. *A HISTORY OF BLACK HOUSING IN SOUTH
AFRICA*. JOHANNESBURG: SOUTH AFRICA FOUNDATION, 1981.)

Urban Health Maps

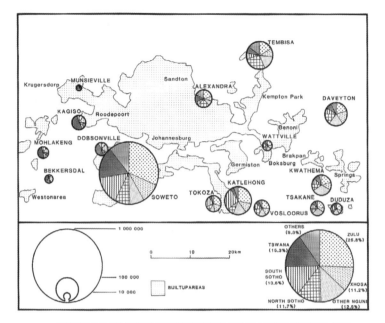

ETHNIC COMPOSITION OF WITWATERSRAND BLACK TOWNSHIPS, 1985,
BASED ON INFORMATION EXTRACTED FROM THE FILES OF THE
CENTRAL STATISTICS SERVICES, PRETORIA, (CHRISTOPHER, A.J. *THE
ATLAS OF APARTHEID.* LONDON AND NEW YORK: ROUTLEDGE, 1994.)

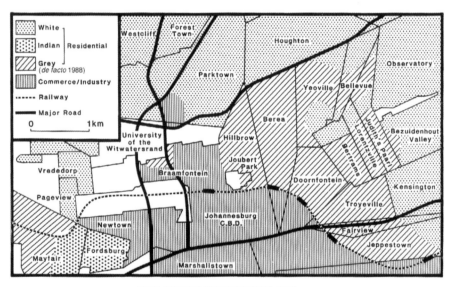

GREY AREAS IN JOHANNESBURG, 1988.
(SOURCE: S.P. RULE "THE EMERGENCE OF A RACIALLY MIXED RESIDEN-
TIAL SUBURB IN JOHANNESBURG: THE DEMISE OF THE APARTHEID
CITY?" *GEOGRAPHICAL JOURNAL* 155: 196-203.)

Sample

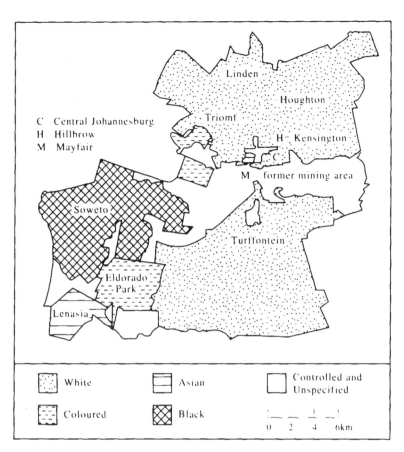

C Central Johannesburg
H Hillbrow
M Mayfair

Legend:
- White
- Coloured
- Asian
- Black
- Controlled and Unspecified

0 2 4 6km

RACIAL ZONING OF JOHANNESBURG, 1987.
(PUBLISHED IN DAVIES, R.J., "THE SPATIAL FORMATION OF THE SOUTH
AFRICAN CITY," *GEOJOURNAL*, SUPPLEMENTARY ISSUE 2 (1981): 59-72.
SOURCED FROM: JOHANNESBURG, 1987, MAP OF GROUP AREAS AND
BLACK TOWNSHIPS. CITY ENGINEER'S DEPARTMENT, JOHANNESBURG)

Urban Health Maps

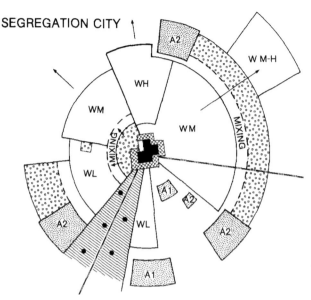

SEGREGATION CITY

WHITE C.B.D. ■ INDIAN C.B.D. ☐ C.B.D. FRAME ▨ INDUSTRIAL ▨
RESIDENTIAL AREAS

White ☐   Economic Status : H - High, M - Middle, L - Low

Indian and/or Coloured   ▨   Economic status not differentiated

African ▨   Barracks Compounds   ● A1 -Municipal Township A2 - Informal housing

Zones of racial mixing - MIXING   Domestic servant quarters not shown

(SOURCE: R.J. DAVIES, "THE SPATIAL FORMATION OF THE SOUTH AFRICAN CITY,"
GEOJOURNAL, SUPPLEMENTARY ISSUE 2 (1981): 59-72.)

The diagram for the Segregation City explains the evolution of the spatial distribution of different racial groups in the settlement patterns of South African
cities. During this period, the spatial organization of ethnic and social groups in
the city was sometimes imposed, but was also the result of voluntary segregation between different groups. In contrast, the Apartheid City represents a
comprehensive, policy of social design begun in 1948. The Apartheid government imposed a spatial control that did not allow for flexibility and instituted a
legal framework for segregation of ethnic groups.

Sample

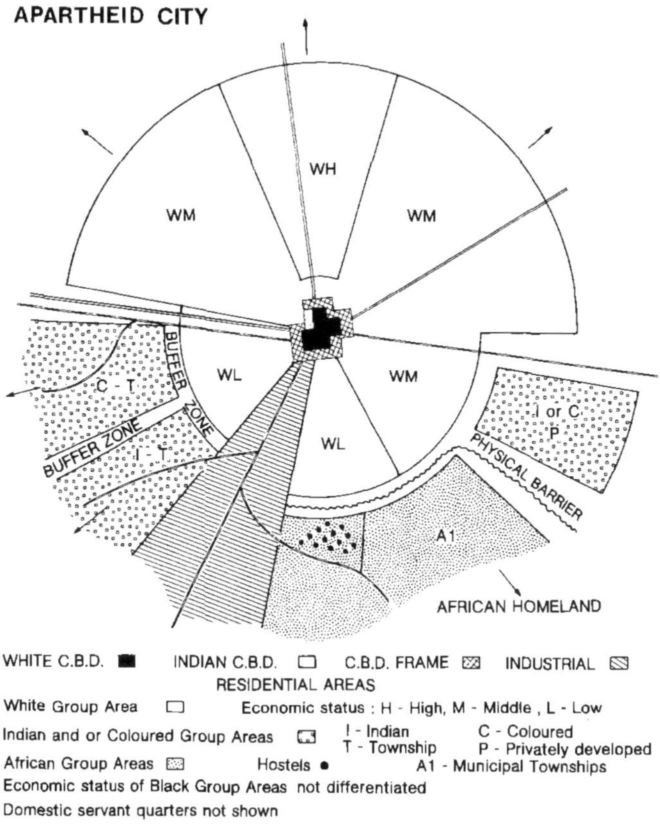
APARTHEID CITY
WH
WM
WM
WL
WM
WL
C - T
BUFFER ZONE
BUFFER ZONE
I - T
I or C
P
PHYSICAL BARRIER
A1
AFRICAN HOMELAND
WHITE C.B.D.
INDIAN C.B.D.
C.B.D. FRAME
INDUSTRIAL
RESIDENTIAL AREAS
White Group Area
Economic status : H - High, M - Middle , L - Low
Indian and or Coloured Group Areas
I - Indian
T - Township
C - Coloured
P - Privately developed
African Group Areas
Hostels
A1 - Municipal Townships
Economic status of Black Group Areas not differentiated
Domestic servant quarters not shown

(SOURCE: R.J. DAVIES, "THE SPATIAL FORMATION OF THE SOUTH AFRICAN CITY," *GEOJOURNAL*, SUPPLEMENTARY ISSUE 2 (1981): 59-72.)

The Apartheid City outlines both the ownership and occupancy of different areas of the city, always prioritizing the white population's advantage in both proximity to employment and land tenure. The white business district at the core of the city was surrounded by Indian or Chinese business districts. Moving outward, white residential districts surrounded the central area. A buffer zone, which could include empty land, physical barriers or industrial zones, would separate the white residential from African, Indian and Coloured Settlements at the periphery. The apartheid zoning prioritized the policy over the rights of land ownership, though this policy nearly always favored the white population.

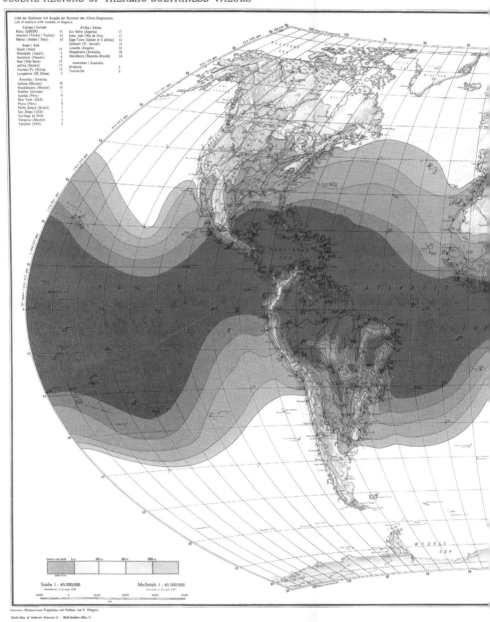

GLOBAL REGIONS OF THERMIC SULTRINESS VALUES
(RODENWALDT, ERNST AND HELMUT J. JUSTATZ, EDS. *WORLD ATLAS OF EPIDEMIC DISEASE.*
HAMBURG: U.S. NAVY BUREAU OF MEDICINE AND SURGERY, 1952.)

130

Sample

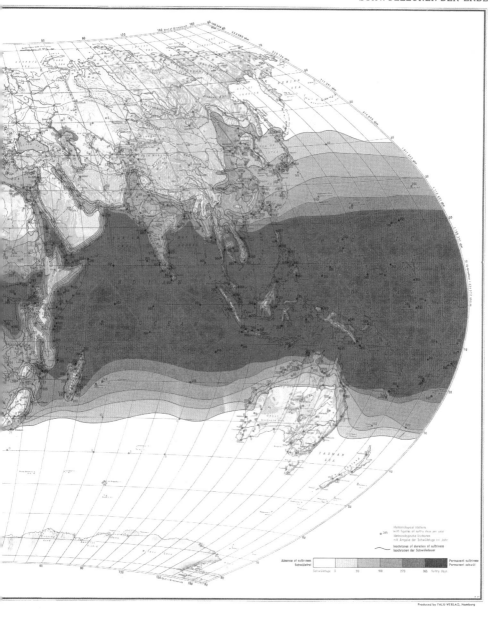

Urban Health Maps

AFRICAN REGION OF THERMIC SULTRINESS VALUES
(RODENWALDT, ERNST AND HELMUT J. JUSTATZ, EDS.
WORLD ATLAS OF EPIDEMIC DISEASE. HAMBURG: U.S. NAVY
BUREAU OF MEDICINE AND SURGERY, 1952.)

132

Sample

Case Studies

Maps and research by Allison Schwartz

Chris Hani Baragwanath Hospital

Soweto
Originally built 1941

The hospital is locally infamous for its sprawling campus and overburdened facilities. What began as a British military hospital, Chris Hani Baragwanath Hospital has grown to become what is currently the largest hospital in the Southern Hemisphere and the main public hospital to serve the population of Soweto. Founded in 1941 as the Royal Imperial Hospital, Baragwanath was built as a series of military barracks and operated by the British until the South African government purchased the hospital in 1948. At this time, the government transferred the non-European division of the Johannesburg hospital and renamed the facilities after John Albert Baragwanath, the original Cornish settler on the land. The name of famous activist Chris Hani was incorporated in 1997, though the hospital is known locally as "Bara."

The walled campus of the hospital contains a maze of buildings that have been adapted over time to serve the needs of the hospital. The adaptive use of the buildings over time shows the resource fulness of the hospital administrators but also reveals the challenges of the pressure on the South African public medical system, as made evident in the expansive hospital and its crowded conditions. While the segregation of white and non-white patients is no longer official policy, the new inequality in health treatment occurs in the current large disparity in the quality of private and public health care in South Africa. For those who can afford to buy into a private health care system, there are

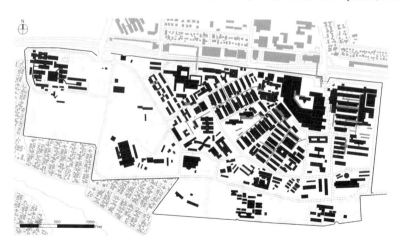

DRAWN FROM 2013 GOOGLE EARTH IMAGERY

high-quality facilities and well-staffed hospitals and clinics. While for those without the money to buy into the private system, the public health care sector is deficient in both its facilities and staffing. Since apartheid, South Africa has faced a brain drain of both doctors and nurses out of the country and to the private health care sector within the country. As a result, only 27 percent of the country's general practitioners work in the public sector and are responsible for treating 82 percent of the country's population.

Bara hospital served as the primary hospital for the black population in Johannesburg during apartheid and the only hospital in all of Soweto. During this time, the majority of nurses were black, but were overseen by white doctors and administrators. The hospital was part of the limited public health care system overseen by the state and, along with thirteen clinics, provided health care for the entire population of Soweto as well as blacks living in other areas of the city. The hospital has also served as an academic teaching hospital, and a large number of South African doctors passed through the hospital during their training.

After the fall of apartheid, Bara continued to serve as the primary public hospital for all of Soweto and many of the surrounding informal settlements. Despite Bara's large size, the hospital has been overwhelmed by the demand for medical services and limited resources to treat patients since the time of its formation, with accounts of high patient counts since 1947. Bara has earned a reputation for overcrowding, shortage of staff, and long wait times.

References

Decoteau, Claire Laurier. "The Bio-Politics of HIV/AIDS in Post-Apartheid South Africa." Ph.D. diss., University of Michigan, 2008.

Schreiber, Lorna. *Johannesburg Hospital/Hospitaal 1890–1990*. Johannesburg: Johannesburg Hospital Board, 1990.

Lane, Charles. "The Bloodied Country." *The New Republic* 210 (10), 20.

AERIAL VIEW OF THE BARAGWANATH HOSPITAL, CIRCA 1950

BARAGWANATH HOSPITAL ENTRANCE IN 2007 BEFORE RENOVATION

BARAGWANATH HOSPITAL BARRACK BUILDINGS

Case Studies

Hillbrow Health Precinct

The Hillbrow Health Precinct represents a concerted effort to revive an abandoned and underused part of the city to benefit an underserved high-risk population. Hillbrow's many residents live without sufficient access to medical resources. The extremely high-density area is largely a low-income population of residents, many of whom are illegal immigrants who do not have access to non-emergency medical treatment. Hillbrow also has a high occurrence of crime, violence, prostitution, sexually transmitted diseases, and violence toward women. As a result of Hillbrow's high-density and high-risk population, the renovation of the precinct will provide much-needed treatment for the surrounding population.

The precinct is composed of a patchwork of health care buildings and supporting facilities that have been built over time. The first health-related buildings on the site were built in the late 1800s, with others added over the years, as new facilities were needed for the South African Institute for Medical Research (SAIMR) and Hillbrow Hospital. Many of the existing buildings on the site were built before World War II and are classified as historically significant structures. The Hillbrow Hospital was decommissioned in 1998, leaving many buildings abandoned, and has since fallen into disrepair.

The precinct currently contains functioning health care facilities and abandoned buildings with illegally squatting occupants directly adjacent to one another. Recent efforts have been made to implement a site plan that reintegrates the area with the city grid by creating new open areas and removing a number of structures in order to make spaces usable for the operation of health care facilities. The Shandukani project, for example, was an abandoned structure renovated to provide much-needed treatment for women and children living in Hillbrow. The renovation attempted to preserve or reuse as much as possible of the existing heritage building, with the additions clearly distinguished by contrasting material and style. Due to spatial limitations, outdoor areas adjacent to the building provide supplemental waiting space for patients. In this way, the creation of public open space throughout the site expands the potential to treat patients as well as improve the comfort of people using the site.

The improvements to the site have also emphasized the benefit of improved way-finding. Due to the many small buildings on the site, health treatment is often fragmented, requiring patients to travel between buildings in order to meet with health practitioners, receive counseling, and access pharmaceuticals. Many patients were discouraged or confused in the dispersal of health services and often did not complete their treatment partially for this reason. Improved signage and clearer passageways between the dispersed services have increased the percentage of patients receiving complete treatment.

References

Bremner, Lindsay. "Mobile Johannesburg." In *In the Life of Cities*, Mohsen Mostavi, ed. Baden: Lars Müller, 2012.

Schreiber, Lorna. *Johannesburg Hospital/Hospitaal 1890–1990*. Johannesburg: Johannesburg Hospital Board, 1990.

Drawn from 2013 Google Earth Imagery.

A. National Council for Occupational Health
B. National Health Laboratory Services
C. State Forensic Chemical Laboratories
D. Johannesburg Mortuary
E. Shandukani
F. Wits reproductive Health and HIV Institute
G. National Blood Transfusion Center
H. Hillbrow Community Health Center
I. Hillbrow Hospital
J. Johannesburg Medical-Legal Center

139

Case Studies

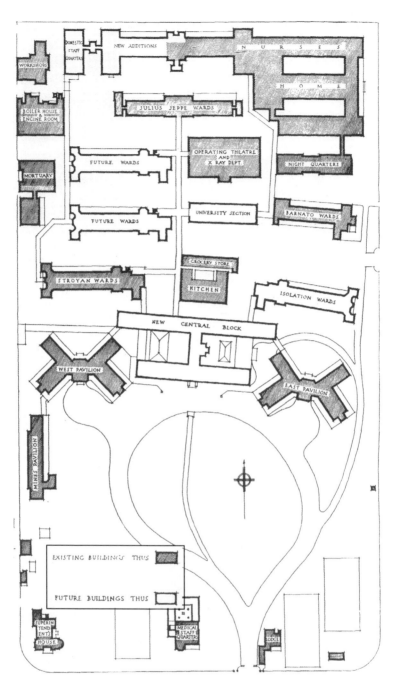

BLOCK PLAN OF JOHANNESBURG HOSPITAL SHOWING THE BUILDINGS
THAT EXISTED IN 1932 (SHADED BLOCKS) AND THOSE BUILDINGS THAT
WERE PLANNED LATER (OPEN BLOCKS)

AERIAL VIEW OF JOHANNESBURG HOSPITAL
BRANCHES, 1935

Key to Aerial View:
Transvaal Memorial Hospital for Children
1. Main Building
2. Observation Ward
3. Nurses' Home
4. Ward Blocks

Queen Victoria Hospital
5. Main Building and Nurses' Home
6. Nurses' Home Extensions
7. Ward Blocks
8. Isolation Ward

Fever Hospital
9. Main Building and Nurses' Home
10. Observation Ward
11. Ward Blocks
12. Laundry
13. Native Compound
14. Night Nurses' Quarters
15. Government Chemical Laboratory

Case Studies

DECOMMISSIONED HILLBROW HOSPITAL

COVERED PASSAGEWAY BETWEEN MEDICAL FACILITIES

143

Case Studies

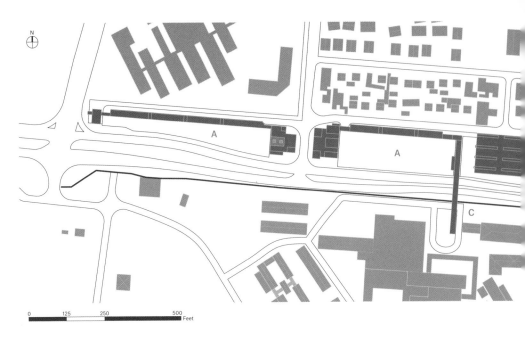

Baragwanath Transport Interchange and Traders Market

Diepsloot, Soweto
Designed by Ludwig Hansen/Urban Solutions Architects and Urban Designers

The interchange consists of a system of buildings that serve the circulation of both people and taxis. Replacing ad hoc structures and an informal vendor market, the new interchange sits on a 1.3-kilometer linear site and consists of taxi-ranking facilities, markets, waiting shelters, and restrooms. The concrete structures provide covered spaces for a series of taxi queues organized to facilitate the unloading and loading of passengers organized by the different destinations and travel routes. Covered market space provides stalls for retailers, and informal vendors line passageways and sidewalks selling food and other goods to commuters and those visiting or working at the hospital. These services respond to the high flow of traffic through the site, which has become the largest taxi-ranking station in Soweto. Nearly 70 percent of all Soweto commuters use the Baragwanath Interchange, switching from Soweto taxi routes to around Johannesburg.

The growth of this expansive busing system responds to historic transportation conditions in Johannesburg. Pre-apartheid public transportation infrastructure heavily favored white areas, leaving most townships without access to the Central Business District and its employment opportunities, resulting in the emergence of a bus system known as Kombi taxis. Private minibuses that operate on fixed routes throughout the city make up the taxi system. The taxis began as an informal solution to the shortage of transportation options but have developed into a loosely organized

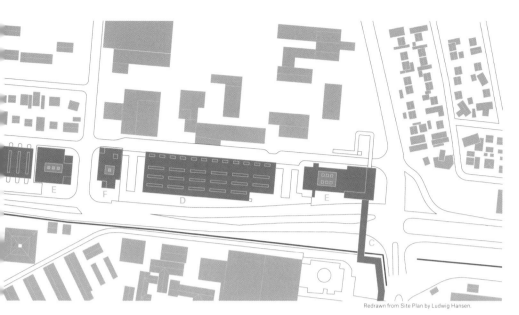

Redrawn from Site Plan by Ludwig Hansen.

A Taxi Holding D Taxi Ranking
B Bus Holding E Market
C Bridge to Hospital F Admin

transportation network through and beyond Johannesburg operating on fixed commuter corridors (long and short distance) and charging fares fixed by local taxi associations. Despite recent attempts to improve civic public transport infrastructure with a new rail and bus lines, of all public transport rides in Johannesburg, 72 percent are made by kombi taxis, 9 percent by bus, 19 percent by rail. The kombi taxi is by far the most commonly used form of public transport and plays a critical role in the lives of the majority of commuters, particularly in poor communities. More than 12,000 minibus taxis serve commuters within Johannesburg and farther into neighboring cities and regions

The taxi rank also provides bridged access to Chris Hani Baragwanath Hospital, which is located directly across the street. Ramped passages bring pedestrians across the heavy traffic road that separates the interchange and hospital. The two bridges serve as the only pedestrian gateways to the hospital. Through these access points, the majority of the hospital's patients, visitors, and staff stream in and out. Because of the Interchange's position in linking commuters to greater Johannesburg and pedestrians to Chris Hani Baragwanath Hospital, the interchange plays an important position in the lives of much of Soweto's population.

References

Deckler, Thorsten and Anne Graupner, Henning Rasmuss eds., *Contemporary South African Architecture in a Landscape of Transition*. Cape Town: Double Story Books, 2006.

VIEW OF TRANSPORT INTERCHANGE FROM SOUTH OVERLOOKING
OLD POTCH ROAD AND DIEPSLOOT IN THE BACKGROUND
(PHOTOGRAPH: LUDWIG HANSEN)

TAXI RANK AND INFORMAL MARKETS BEFORE CONSTRUCTION OF
NEW BUILDINGS (PHOTOGRAPH: LUDWIG HANSEN)

END OF TAXI RANK WITH RAMP CONNECTING
TO BARAGWANATH HOSPITAL

COVERED WAITING AREAS FOR PASSENGERS WAITING FOR TAXIS
(PHOTOGRAPH: LUDWIG HANSEN)

Case Studies

CHRIS HANI BARAGWANATH HOSPITAL

DR GEORGE MUKHARI HOSPITAL

HELEN JOSEPH HOSPITAL

TEMBISA HOSPITAL

RAHIMA MOOSA HOSPITAL

SEBOKENG HOSPITAL

EDENVALE GENERAL HOSPITAL

KOPANONG HOSPITAL

LERATONG HOSPITAL

MAMELODI HOSPITAL

149

Case Studies

The urban housing shortage in South Africa has been a consistent issue for both the apartheid and post-apartheid governments. The South African housing problem persists due to a number of complex conditions that include historical housing patterns planned under apartheid and limited funds to construct housing. New national housing programs have provided many new units, but the shortage persists as existing need remains unmet and immigrants continue to move to the city from rural areas and neighboring countries.

Generic blocks of single-family homes comprise the iconic image of the low-density township. This housing is often generalized as the "matchbox house" due to the repetitive shape and construction materials. In fact, a number of housing designs were used over the years that explored different configurations and densities. The development of the government-housing programs explored different layouts, but the majority of the research emphasized low costs and efficiency in construction. The most common house constructed in all black townships was the $^{51}/_6$ prototype, a four-room 40.4-square-meter house. Many of the matchbox houses have since been expanded and personalized by residents; informal housing is often mixed into the neighborhoods.

The limited size and low-density arrangement of the non-white townships was an intentional design decision by the apartheid government. Influenced by principles of the English New Towns, the townships were to be limited to a population of 1,500 and a gross density of between thirty and forty persons per acre. The single-family, four-room houses that were built were nearly always overcrowded with multiple family members sleeping in each room. To achieve this mass delivery of housing, empty land on the city's fringe was transformed into dormitory communities. Most of what eventually became Soweto was constructed this way. Though the planning of these neighborhoods was based on the model of the Garden City, the South African implementation provided insufficient infrastructure. Apartheid policy created the fictional construct that Africans in Johannesburg were migrant labor, staying temporarily in the city before returning to their rural homelands. As a result, the new township neighborhoods were built to achieve ethnic segregation and maintain control of the black, urban population, but these new neighborhoods had insufficient, or entirely lacked, open, cultural, or retail spaces, as well as public transportation and secondary education. Much of this social infrastructure, such as high school, was withheld in order to structure the urban townships as temporary dormitory communities rather than the established cities they were becoming.

Despite the many townships built under national housing policies, the country continues to have a housing shortage due to the growth of urban areas. One of the first issues of the post-apartheid government was to address the severe housing shortage. The National Housing Policy of 1996 mandates that "Everyone has the right to have access to adequate housing" and "The state must take reasonable legislative and other measures, within its available resources, to achieve the progressive realization of this right." Through this Reconstruction and Development Programme

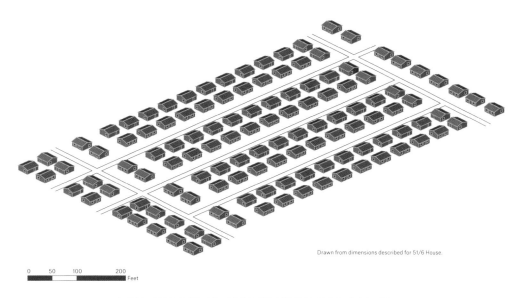

Drawn from dimensions described for 51/6 House.

0   50   100   200
                         Feet

TYPICAL NEIGHBORHOOD OF GOVERNMENT-BUILT HOUSING DRAWN
USING SOWETO NEIGHBORHOOD PLANT AND 51/6 HOUSE

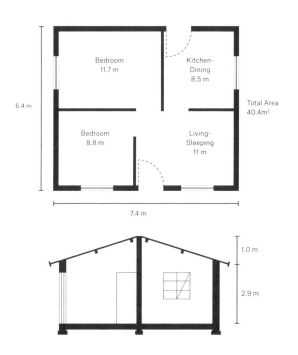

PLAN AND SECTION OF THE STANDARD 51/6 HOUSE, THE MOST
COMMONLY BUILT HOUSE FOR BLACK TOWNSHIPS IN THE EARLY 1950s
(REDRAWN FROM MORRIS, *HISTORY OF BLACK HOUSING*)

PANORAMA OF SOWETO IN THE 1960s
(PHOTOGRAPH FROM MORRIS,
HISTORY OF BLACK HOUSING)

51/6 HOUSES UNDER CONSTRUCTION IN MAPETLA
AND PHIRI (SOWETO) 1960s
(PHOTOGRAPH FROM MORRIS,
HISTORY OF BLACK HOUSING)

(RDP), the government created subsidies to partially finance the construction of primarily single-family housing. The typical 36-square-meter RDP house sits on a 250-square-meter lot in newly established neighborhoods. Typical houses have an open-plan bedroom, lounge, and kitchen with separate bathroom, and include basic services of running water, sewage, and electricity. Occupants of RDP housing have secure land tenure, which ensures security of occupation without threat of forced evictions.

The RDP houses have partially relieved the national housing shortage, with approximately 2.3 million houses built between 1994 and 2009, but has also brought new problems. Partially this is because RDP housing is often indistinguishable from housing built during apartheid and replicates many of the same problems caused by the low-density neighborhoods and simple, often low-quality constructed housing. Many of these new communities are frequently incomplete, leaving many without access to properly functioning infrastructure, schools, or health care. These dormitory communities are distant from work opportunities, and residents are financially burdened by the cost of transportation. Further, their location at the outskirts of the city is often in proximity to the mine dumps with possibly dangerous components in the soil and airborne dust. The cheaply constructed housing has no mechanical ventilation system, so residents are forced to open windows and allow the mine dust into their homes.

References

Chipkin, Clive M. *Johannesburg Transition: Architecture & Society From 1950*. Johannesburg: STE Publishers, 2008.

Christopher, A.J., "Racial Land Zoning in Urban South Africa." *Land Use Policy*, Vol. 14, No. 4 (1997): 311–23.

Davies, R.J., "The Spatial Formation of the South African City," *GeoJournal*, Supplementary Issue, 2: 59–72.

Mabin, Alan. "Reconstruction and the Making of Urban Planning in 20th-Century South Africa." In *Blank: Architecture, Apartheid, and After*, edited by

Hilton Judin and Ivan Vladislavic. Rotterdam: NAi Publishers, March 2, 1999.

Morris, Pauline. *A History of Black Housing in South Africa*. Johannesburg: South Africa Foundation, 1981.

National Housing Policy, Section 26, Constitution of the Republic of South Africa, 1996.

Schwartz

HOUSING ANALYSIS OF NEIGHBORHOOD NORTH OF BARAGWANATH
TRANSPORT INTERCHANGE AND HOSPITAL

FORMAL HOUSING

1 2 3 4

INFORMAL HOUSING

5 6 7

TRADITIONAL HOUSING

8

CLASSIFICATION OF HOUSING

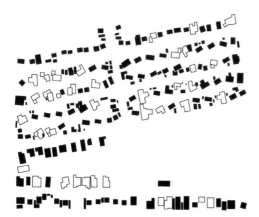

SINGLE

COMBINATION

HOUSING TYPES

153

Case Studies

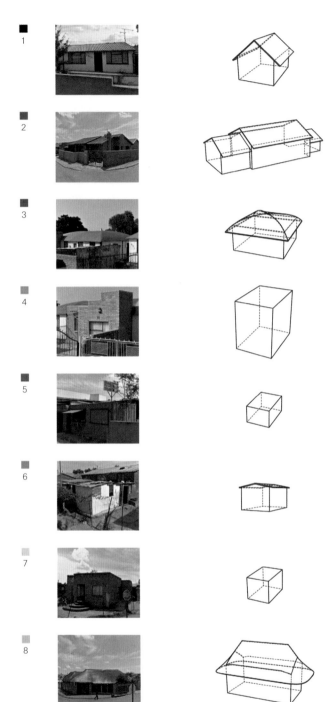

SINGLE HOUSING TYPES

Schwartz

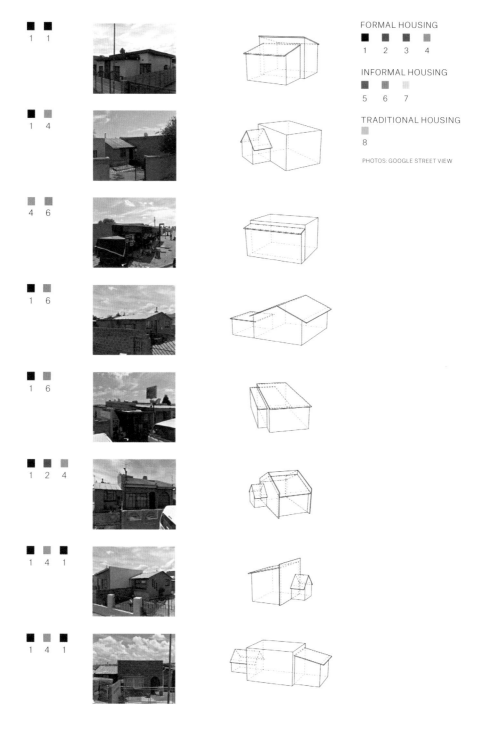

PHOTOS: GOOGLE STREET VIEW

COMBINATION HOUSING TYPES

155

Case Studies

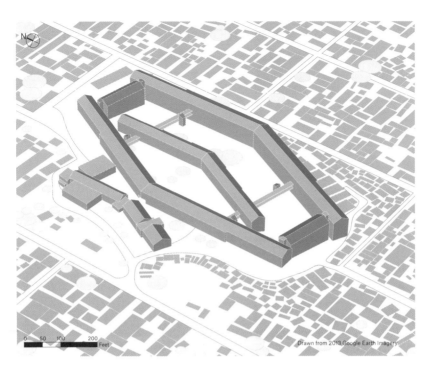

Women's Hostel

Alexandra
Completed 1971

Hostels represent the height of the apartheid policy's attempt to control the black population. Housing for working men in Johannesburg began to be transferred to single-sex dormitory housing in Soweto built under the Native (Urban Areas) Amendment Act of 1955. The hostel typology instituted an architecture of control to disrupt the family structure by segregating male and female workers through the use of a building designed for optimal surveillance and minimal personal space. In 1963 a decision was made to rehouse the entire population of Alexandra in single-sex hostels and eliminate all family housing. Twenty-five hostels were to be built in Alexandra, each to house more than 2,500 workers in an attempt to control the black worker population through division in single-sex housing. The enormous diamond-shaped structure of the Women's Hostel is composed of linear bars of dormitories with shared bath and kitchen facilities. At its extremes, the hostel is 750 feet by 400 feet, roughly the same area as a Manhattan block.

Only three of these hostels were built in Alexandra: the Madala Men's Hostel, built in 1971; the Nobuthie Men's Hostel, built in 1972; and the Helen Joseph Women's Hostel, built in 1971. The two men's hostels have since been converted into apartments, but the women's hostel continues to operate as a dormitory, partially as a result of the hostel's affordable rates, security, and favorable location. The hostel has continued to be popular despite the restrictive conditions.

Schwartz

ALEXANDRA HOSTELS, 1972
(PHOTOGRAPH FROM MORRIS, *HISTORY OF BLACK HOUSING*)

In the case of the women's hostel, the community of women and children inhabitants has adapted the imposed architecture of control into an operational system that allows for self-policing of the facilities. The hostels have dealt with declining facilities, continuous maintenance problems, and conflicts among residents.

Despite dedicated residents, an aging building combined with local politics and challenges of operating housing exclusively for women have recently brought attention to the hostel. The SABC News story from August 30, 2012, reports on recent internal disagreements between residents concerning the policy that does not permit boys older than twelve to live in the women's hostel, as boys of even younger ages have been forced out, continuing the legacy of apartheid disrupting the family structure. Additionally, maintenance issues with the hostel's rubbish, sewage drainage, and inadequate fire prevention equipment have also received media attention and outcry from residents.

References

Chipkin, Clive M. *Johannesburg Transition: Architecture & Society From 1950*. Johannesburg: STE Publishers, 2008.

Morris, Pauline. *A History of Black Housing in South Africa*. Johannesburg: South Africa Foundation, 1981.

Faraday Market and Transport Interchange

Johannesburg
Architect: Albonico + Sack Architects and Urban Designers
with MMA Architects

The new transportation and market facilities have revived a decaying area of central Johannesburg with programming tailored to the commuting population. The multinodal transportation center replaces the historic Faraday railway station with a new interchange catering to the prevalent mode of transportation by the majority of Johannesburg's commuters—the taxi. The building accommodates the taxi ranks but also includes gathering and office space for taxi-rank operators and drivers.

This project seeks to improve transportation infrastructure through connections between taxis, buses, and commuter trains. Long underserved from the times of the apartheid goverment, black commuters coming from urban townships and rural areas often resorted to informal transportation options due to the paucity of public transportation connecting commercial centers with employment to the black-designated residential areas. Transportation options are now more diverse, but many taxis and buses pick up passengers on the side of the road or beneath highway overpasses, as was the case of the Faraday station prior to the new construction. The new station provides a ranking area for taxis and buses, a connection to the train station, covered waiting areas, and retail intended for commuters.

The new interchange also includes space for muti traders in order to replace the informal stalls that surrounded the previous taxi rank area. The traditional practice of muti consists of plant and animal products that are cultivated specifically for this purpose. The traditional medicine market facilities at Faraday provide space for hundreds of muti healers and traders that offer consultations on wellness, as well as provide traditional healing supplies brought in from other regions of the country. Indigenous traditional healing was legally prohibited during apartheid, labeled witchcraft, divination, or sorcery. There was no attempt to integrate traditional healing beliefs with biomedical health care in the official health system. Despite the illegality, traditional healing persisted in the urban townships and rural Bantustans throughout apartheid. In the post-apartheid state, attempts have been made to merge traditional healing with biomedical health care.

The architectural framework of the station and market were designed for flexibility to incorporate the requirements of the vendors. The success of the project can be seen in the overflowing stalls, and attraction of additional vendors who are moving into surrounding lots to expand the market. This project has succeeded in bringing new life to the area and in developing a program specifically tailored to the needs of commuters from townships.

References

Deckler, Thorsten and Anne Graupner, Henning Rasmuss eds., *Contemporary South African Architecture in a Landscape of Transition.* Cape Town: Double Story Books, 2006.

Decoteau, Claire Laurier. "The Bio-Politics of HIV/AIDS in Post-Apartheid South Africa." Ph.D. diss., University of Michigan, 2008.

Mda, Lizeka. "City Quarters: Civic Spine, Faraday Station, KwaMayiMayi, and Ponte City." In *Blank: Architecture, Apartheid, and After*, edited by Hilton Judin and Ivan Vladislavic. Rotterdam: NAi Publishers, 1999.

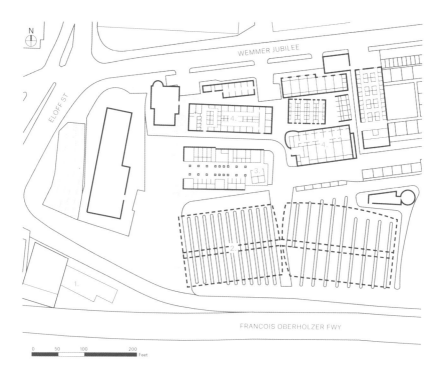

1. FARRADAY METRORAIL STATION   3. RETAIL
2. TAXI RANK   4. VENDOR STALLS

REDRAWN FROM 2013 GOOGLE EARTH IMAGERY AND THORSTEN
DECKLER, ANNE GRAUPNER, HANNIG RASMUSS EDS., *CONTEMPORARY
SOUTH AFRICAN ARCHITECTURE IN A LANDSCAPE OF TRANSITION*

COVERED TAXI RANKING AREA

STALLS OF TRADITIONAL MEDICINE HEALERS
AND VENDORS

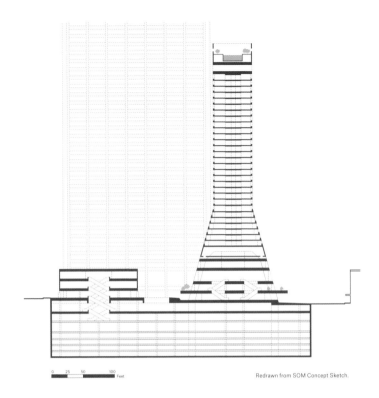

0 25 50 100
Feet

Redrawn from SOM Concept Sketch.

Carlton Centre

Central Business District
Designed by Skidmore Owings and Merill
Construction completed in 1973

The center is composed of a fifty-story office tower, thirty-story hotel, shopping mall, commercial arcade, park, and underground parking. At 730 feet tall, the commercial office tower was both Africa's tallest building and the world's highest reinforced-concrete building. The concrete brutal style is representative of the international architectural aesthetics at the time of its construction, symbolizing Johannesburg's place as a global African city and monumentalizing Johannesburg's economic growth in the 1970s.

References

Chipkin, Clive M. *Johannesburg Transition: Architecture & Society From 1950*. Johannesburg: STE Publishers, 2008

Chipkin, Clive. "The Great Apartheid Building Boom: The Transformation of Johannesburg in the 1960s." In *Blank: Architecture, Apartheid, and After,* edited by Hilton Judin and Ivan Vladislavic. Rotterdam: NAi Publishers, 1999.

CARLTON CENTRE WITH MINES IN THE FOREGROUND
(PHOTOGRAPH: EZRA STOLLER)

CARLTON CENTRE FROM THE STREET
(PHOTOGRAPH: EZRA STOLLER)

161
—
Case Studies

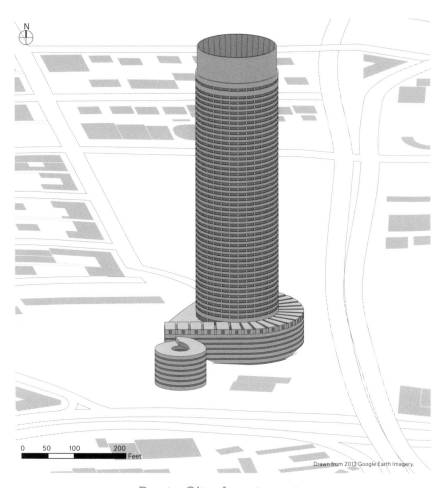

Drawn from 2013 Google Earth Imagery.

0   50   100   200
|————————————————| Feet

Ponte City Apartments

Hillbrow
Architects: Mannie Feldman, Manfred Hermer, and Rodney Grosskopff
Construction completed 1975

The fifty-four-story cylindrical apartment tower was built at the height of Johannesburg's prosperity, imagined as a self-sufficient "city" at the edge of the at the time trendy Hillbrow neighborhood. The tower is the tallest residential building in Africa with an inner, uncovered atrium running the full height of the building. A base of amenities and retail spaces were envisioned to serve the daily needs of the building's residents.

As the end of apartheid drew near and whites fled from the rapidly changing Hillbrow, most of the building's original intended tenants left, rents dropped, and new low-rent occupants moved in. The building eventually fell into disrepair and had many squatters. The maintenance of the building

Schwartz

was increasingly neglected, and eventually there were several floors of debris piled within the inner atrium. As a result of the publicized state of the tower, Ponte City became a symbol of Hillbrow's high immigrant population, significant crime problems, and urban neglect.

The fate of the tower has gone through numerous iterations, including discussions in the late 1990s, to turn the tower into a prison. This proposal was a result of the Ministry of Correctional Services invitation to American architect Paul Silver, an expert on prison design, to consider locations for constructing a new jail in Johannesburg. He settled on the idea of transforming Ponte City into the world's tallest prison facility with legal courts in the planned commercial base and cells in the tower. By incorporating all elements of the correctional system in one building, the need to transport criminals after their arrest would be eliminated. This transformation never occurred, and the tower's ownership was transferred.

Ponte's new owners have refurbished apartments and public spaces as well as restricted access to the tower and improved the security for residents. While diverging from the utopian vision of the tower's architects, units are now occupied mostly by students and middle-class Africans, and the commercial and shared spaces are currently being renovated. Ponte City has entered a new chapter in its history.

References

Hartford, Anna. "Ponte City." *n+1* magazine. June 14, 2013. http://nplusonemag.com/ponte-city.
Mda, Lizeka. "City Quarters: Civic Spine, Faraday Station, KwaMayiMayi, and Ponte City." In *Blank: Architecture, Apartheid, and After,* edited by

Hilton Judin and Ivan Vladislavic. Rotterdam: NAi Publishers, March 2, 1999.
O'Loughlin, Ed. "Skyscraper Jail for Sky-High Crime." *The Christian Science Monitor,* April 27, 1998.

APARTMENTS ARE ACCESSED
BY CIRCULAR CORRIDOR

THE REAR SIDE OF THE BILLBOARD
CROWNING THE TOWER

163

Case Studies

Symposium

The Intersection Between Urban Health and Architecture

Panel Discussion

April 22, 2013

Hilary Sample
Associate professor, GSAPP, principal MOS Architects

Jay Siebenmorgen
Design principal, NBBJ

Vishaan Chakrabarti
CURE, associate professor of real estate, Columbia University,
principal, SHoP Architects

Rich Dallam
FAIA, partner, NBBJ

Joanna Frank
Director of active design, DDC, NYC

Thomas De Monchaux
Adjunct assistant professor, GSAPP

Karen Lee, M.D.
Deputy director of the New York City Department
of Mental Health and Hygiene

Gina Lovasi
Assistant professor of epidemiology,
Columbia University Mailman School of Public Health

Leah Meisterlin
Term professor, Barnard College,
partner, Office: MG

Marc Norman
Urban planner, UPSTATE, Syracuse University

Joan Saba
AIA; FACHA; partner, NBBJ

Hilary Sample   One of the first things Sandro Galea, chairman of epidemiology at the Mailman School, said when he came to meet with the students is that epidemiologists don't like the term of *stress*. Gina, could you elaborate on this? For architects it means many things. It can be assigned to structures, indicate stress on urban infrastructures, and other issues. There are multiple ways into the term for an architecture student.

Gina Lovasi   One of the reasons that we don't like *stress* is because the components of it are so important and so different from each other. It is both a source of health problems and a symptom of health problems. I think that the criticism of that term is because it is hard to measure stress when it is such a mix. Where we can more readily measure social inequalities or look at symptoms of stress as reported by individuals or look at depression or coping behaviors. So I think that we would like to unpack and separate stress into distinct components, some of which may be experienced as a consequence of the built environment.

Thomas De Monchaux   That reminds me that just yesterday, by coincidence, a dear friend of mine went to a conference on the theme of fatigue, and the attitude toward fatigue is very much what we say about stress. We use these words casually as if there were some ideal preferable state in which neither of these things existed. We want a world without fatigue. We want a world without stress. One of the points of the conference that she's at is that we are going to be stressed all the time, that stress is part of our continual condition. It is not some other state that has to be carefully handled. It has to be incorporated, and embodied, and in a weird way welcomed in the way a well-engineered building is under constant stress every minute of its life, but the stress is being focused, managed, and directed. So the rhetoric of this conference is: let's be stressed, but let's be really well-stressed. Let's be fatigued, but let's be really well-fatigued. The meeting that I most appreciated hearing about was one where the presenter was pointing out that what we think of as the absence of stress, what we think of as luxury, relaxation, and rest in today's lifestyle is often actually a real stressor, like long periods of being sedentary or diets high in fat and sugar. These things can cause a kind of relief but are actually huge stressors.

Gina Lovasi   I think that's really interesting. The income of a neighborhood is such a strong predictor of health outcomes but we don't know why. One of my thesis students from last year looked at whether having a certain genotype affects whether your heart rate goes up in stressful situations like public speaking, and if that modifies the relationship between being in a low-income neighborhood and having cardiac arrest. She found that the high-risk genotype intensified that relationship between low-income neighborhoods and cardiac arrest. The idea that we could try to understand why people are different in responding to different types of environments is really

Urban Health and Architecture

a good direction that we have the chance to explore now. Also, I like the idea of good stress because we know we need to have stress at some times in order to get us to act and do what we need to do, but there's also the idea that if stress continues without pause or reprieve it builds up and becomes problematic. It becomes a contributor to cardiovascular disease particularly.

Rich Dallam   There is a brain scientist that we've worked with for the last several years who wrote a book called *Brain Rules* and it supports your point. Basically, he said that humans evolved over millions of years under constant stress, so we are actually built for stress and stressors in the environment. The question is how you react to those stressors. Part of what we've looked at in the stress equation is that you have to have a raised physiological response, you have to perceive it as adverse and then you have to see it as out of your control. So thinking about this from a design perspective, the issue is: how you can provide choice so that you can create some form of control in the environment? And how do you change the conditions where something that is exhilarating to one person causes someone else to recoil, where the perception of stress differs?

Thomas De Monchaux   I think the parameters of demand and control are really good ones for evaluating the performance of the built environment even if they cannot be necessarily quantified or measured in ways that you might wish. If you think about what a building does, it's this weird choreography of control and demand over experience. A good building necessarily limits your options, reduces your control, curating your experience in a certain way. It also, at least in theory, gives you the opportunity to make empowering choices.

Marc Norman   I'm thinking now that at my center we've spent the last six months actually trying to create fatigue and stress in a good way. Because in a very poor neighborhood, what you would think would be pretty stress-free—lots of unemployment, lots of sedentary sort of individuals—has horrible health outcomes. So when we started looking at redesigning the street, we tried to think about ways in which people could inadvertently exercise as they moved down the street or take the long way or figure out ways to stay outside longer. I didn't think about the control aspects of it, of "I don't have a job" or "I don't have a place to go." If you don't actually have any control over that, then you are creating an environment of stress in addition to your sedentary lifestyle. I think that design can play a huge role if we figure out those kinds of subtle ways, and I imagine Joanna has some very interesting ways of thinking about this as well.

Joanna Frank   Yes. What New York City has been doing for the last six or seven years is really looking at ways to change the built environment, understanding that the built environment historically has played a massive role in affecting public health. To take on again as a profession that there is health evidence that architects aren't really used to,

HILLBROW,
JOHANNESBURG
(MAP DATA: GOOGLE, 2011)

SOWETO,
JOHANNESBURG
(MAP DATA: GOOGLE, 2012)

ALEXANDRA,
JOHANNESBURG
(MAP DATA: GOOGLE, 2012)

169

Urban Health and Architecture

FINANCIAL DISTRICT, NEW YORK CITY
(MAP DATA: GOOGLE, 2012)

CITY CENTER, COPENHAGEN
(MAP DATA: GOOGLE, 2013)

HARLEM, NEW YORK CITY
(MAP DATA: GOOGLE, 2012)

and that urban planners aren't used to making choices based on evidence. As you said, it's somewhat of a faith-based thing we do here. To have evidence added, then it seems the decision-making is actually not yours. You need to do this because there is evidence that this will make a difference. If you can use this evidence, then this is an interesting way for architects to come at the process. We talk about where to put stairs, how to move people through a building in a way so that they don't know that they are being directed but they are actually directed. We are doing it as a very conscious thing by using all of these different indicators. When we put plantings down a street, people are more likely to walk. When you put benches in a park, people are more likely to walk even though that seems counterintuitive. We can prove that these things make a difference. We do keep having the question: How do we measure success and what is success? It is very difficult to measure public health. It's a massive thing and takes a long time. You want something faster, but, Karen, would you like to talk more about some of the evidence?

Karen Lee   So if you look at the lead causes of death today in the U.S., they are tobacco, obesity, high blood pressure, high sugar, and physical inactivity. Those are the top five. The second, third, and fourth are, of course, all linked together, caused by this equation of insufficient physical activity with unhealthy eating and too much energy intake. These diseases, like heart disease and stroke, for example, have been the leading causes of death in the developed world since the mid-twentieth century. Public health has attempted to raise awareness through health education. I'd say that the awareness of health education has paid off. If you look at New Year's resolutions people want to lose weight, eat better, and exercise more. Yet we know that the behavior changes that are encompassed in those resolutions are not successfully being implemented.

Leah Meisterlin   The rate of change in our environment is, I think, enormously important in managing our stress levels. This applies to both our physical environment and our economic and social environment. Because there is a sad flip side to this in that you could suspect that the stresses of low socioeconomic groups can be accounted for under certain long, institutionalized social structures, and if this could be adjusted, their lives would be less stressful. The changes in our environment both physical and nonphysical in the last fifteen to twenty years have been so pronounced that none of us have been able to evolve fast enough to deal with it. The built environment is a start and a direction to move in but can't alone begin to address this.

Vishaan Chakrabarti   I agree. It can't be the built environment alone, but it's a good place to start. I think that I'm on a slightly different page of Thomas' bible in the sense that I think before we talk about design and planning solving some of these issues, we

Urban Health and Architecture

first need to talk about undoing the enormous amount of damage our professions have collectively done on this issue over the last hundred years.

If you think about the enormous changes that've happened with the way you talk about cities and wellness over the last 100–150 years or so, cities historically have been thought of as a scourge to public health and joy. Urban planners and architects, even those beloved to us like Corb, have worked very hard to tame and change all that. Along with a lot of corporate interests, government interests, the Cold War and lots of other stuff have led to an environment where we spread out our population. We are now spreading out that population worldwide. People say the world is urbanizing, but the world is not urbanizing, the world is suburbanizing with really drastic health effects. To me it's interesting to hear from the professionals in the room who really deal with health. You can find extraordinary amounts of data on the correlation between, let's say, economics and density and certainly the environment and density. It's much harder to find public health data associated with density, yet if you dig, it's there. There's a fair correlation between obesity and commute distance. There's a very interesting Swedish study about the correlation between divorce rates and commute distance, which is associated not just with time but with stress. So you look at that and then take the United States, 12 percent of the zoned land has been zoned densely enough to support mass transit. So the planning profession has actively gone out and created a world that engenders bad health. They didn't do it on purpose, but there were a lot of interests that got us to that point. I just think that at the urbanism scale there is a huge amount of damage to undo before we can even hope that we can design something that is going to make someone reach for an apple.

Marc Norman   I think another crime, well maybe misdemeanor, of modernism is the result of zoning. You want to make a healthier environment, therefore the factories are separated from housing and the housing is separated from the business district. I think in the architectural profession we've done that as well. We are experts in building hospitals, schools, educational facilities, or housing, but what if architects were experts in, let's say, health, and we are designing grocery stores, hospitals, and clinics?

Rich Dallam   I was in Johannesburg a couple of years ago for about two weeks, and the lasting impression I had is that the impoverished population is free, and the empowered, wealthy population is behind razor-ribbon walls. I travel and walk cities, and Johannesburg is one of the few cities that I couldn't walk because of the perception of safety. Our host wouldn't let me go out walking, particularly at night. So isn't that curious, the ones who have less economically have socially vibrant shantytowns that, at some levels of social connection, work? The other ones were absolutely isolated by what I thought was the most horrific expression of paranoia, which has led to horrible stress because they are always worried about someone breaking in and stealing their stuff.

Symposium

Karen Lee   Architecture has one part of the solution in the complexity of issues and complex systems that we need to address. The design of physical space is not the only solution; there are also solutions to be found in the design of our economic and social spheres. Concerning this question of should we be designing to shape behaviors and choices, the reality particularly in evidence-based is playing out that if those designs are actually harmful then there is an ethical obligation to redesign. The other piece is that I don't think it's an "or" approach. For example, there is a top-down way to design, but there are also ways to essentially bring in community inputs and participatory processes in an informed way. So not merely bringing the community together and saying "What do you want?" but rather that same question preceded by a presentation of what we know about the evidence and what we know about how design can shape behaviors, health, etc. So there is a way to empower the community as well as socially design.

Leah Meisterlin   I absolutely agree that the evidence reveals the need to redesign, but the medical analogy breaks down when consistently the built equivalent of the clinical trial is closer to permanent and continually the "subjects," I suppose, of the trial are always the same population. I've had conversations before where people will say that they have new ideas for experimentation in the architecture of public or social housing because it's the best place to experiment because you can design the whole thing, and it's a population most in need. My gut response is that it raises a huge ethical question in that those populations don't get to choose where they live, and they don't get to choose to participate or not to participate. If we are talking about a population whose choices are already diminished, and their diminished choices are having health consequences, then exploiting the fact that they can't choose to participate in our experiments is dangerous. I'm nervous about the analogy when we take it to the experiment extent, but it does raise the ethical question of how many lives get affected by something that we haven't tested and that we won't test on a different population first.

Joan Saba   That's exactly what I was going to comment on, because I think we as architects—and I know from designing health care facilities, love the evidence-based A or B—okay, B, great! We all know that it's so much more messy than that. There is so much more information or understanding that we don't have for this complex organism of whatever it is that we are designing. As architects we are the leaders at recognizing how messy it is. We must take from the community, take from other experts that we can bring in, research, and help inform the client in order to move forward and affect policy for the long term. We should first grab the low-hanging fruit, such as can we have operable windows in a hospital? Or why not? So, how as designers can we lead this change?

Urban Health and Architecture

Karen Lee   Also I think it's important to not equate social well-being and health with health and social services per se. Those services should be there and should be available, but if you were to look at how much of health is actually determined by health care, it is actually a very small portion. If you look at how social services determine social well-being, it is also a very small portion. So those services need to be there, but the conditions of design outside of those services are fundamentally what shape health.

Rich Dallam   You [Vishaan] said something earlier that I thought was important. If you are going to make decisions at different scales, or time frame, it's really important to understand that there are certain things that are going to last for 100 years. If you get those wrong, which was your point earlier, then you've really screwed up. You've screwed things up for a lot of people, and you can't change it easily. But if you look at retail, retail is constantly experimenting and changing things that don't work from a market perspective. They create a very flexible infrastructure that allows them to change and experiment. I think that's an interesting point that is woven through the conversation about what are the big things, who's making those big decisions, and how do we help this design community conform to that? You don't see the design community really interacting with policymakers much. We went to Washington, D.C., and design isn't even on the map. In comparison, we went to Copenhagen, where the design profession, academia, and policymakers all work together. It was such a contrast between Copenhagen and Washington, D.C.

Vishaan Chakrabarti   It's very tough, and I think you put your finger on it that a lot of these issues that impact our population in terms of health at scale are driven by a lot of largely bad policies that flow out of Washington and sometimes are reinforced at the local level. I actually think at the local level there is a lot more intelligence, but it's very hard to get at because, frankly, the design professions in this country, as we've all experienced, have little to no power in the large-scale policy framework of the United States. Again, my favorite thing to punch at is the suburbanization issue, not because of people's choices relative to it but the degree to which the government has created a whole policy framework, from the mortgage interest deduction to highway financing, oil and gas subsidies. There's just this litany, hundreds of billions of dollars annually, but everyone walks around and imagines that the environment we live in today is some type of natural consequence of free choice. It's absolute hogwash. Those are all driven by policy decisions that even well-intentioned lawmakers have no clue about. Largely because we have very little in terms of education about these issues. So even if someone's a brilliant attorney and becomes, say, the president of the United States, they don't necessarily have any tools with which to tackle the physical issues that impact this stuff for a population. As opposed to a lot of other places in the world where I think those tools exist. It certainly points to the European countries, but there has also been some very interesting stuff done in Japan. We are way behind on this.

Symposium

Thomas De Monchaux In terms of being behind or ahead, I'm kind of interested from our urbanist about this dilemma of what the software engineers call the dilemma of legacy systems. We are stuck with all of this existing structure and infrastructure that is a century old or a decade old or a minute old and now has this type of instant obsolescence. One of these existing systems is this invisible policy framework. As designers, what is our attitude to legacy systems? I was speaking with a health care designer, and he has learned never to ask the E.R. surgeon what he wants because what that surgeon will do is in his head go around his existing emergency environment/operation room and will make a series of corrections. So what he'll describe is the corrected version of the legacy system rather than what he has an opportunity to do, which is this kind of rare, ground-up development that could leapfrog with new possibilities. He says it's much easier, ironically, to do this work where there is no existing system.

Gina Lovasi I am thinking about the evidence base that we have that already built fits with what we could do in the future. Any statistics that I do on the existing environment is always going to be different versions of the legacy system and not the reimagined future system that could be the solution. I think we tend to look at the evidence-base to see which solution from what we have already tried could work, but it might not be there. It might be that by studying what we have already done, constrain ourselves to finding what's not working as planned or is causing unexpected problems.

As an example of solutions-focused thinking, some of my work recently has been looking at the tree plantings and trees that we have in New York and how they are distributed in order to try to understand whether the potential physical activity benefits and the potential respiratory health benefits are playing out. It looks like there might be trade-offs rather than co-benefits. The idea had been that we'll plant trees and that will have economic, social, physical activity, and air-quality benefits, and as a result, we should be able to see health benefits in these areas. Concerning physical activity and obesity, we've been working on some other evidence suggests street trees encourage people to walk along the street. On the flip side, we've been doing a Forest Service–funded project on the distribution of street trees and trying to understand what the impact on air quality at the street level. We've assembled new data to see whether the theoretical relationship of more trees to less air pollution holds up. We are still finalizing the results, but it seems like the traffic distribution patterns are much, much more important.

Joanna Frank We are in a very much metrics-driven world of policy in New York City. It's all about numbers and things that you can quantify. It's easier to quantify in a very confined way.

Rich Dallam You are talking about the social experiment on the underprivileged, but there are social experiments happening all the time. Look at an entire generation of

Urban Health and Architecture

oversized homes that were built as single-family that are completely useless. How do you reframe the argument to someone who's got the economic means, whether it's the government, a developer, etc., to do something that has a better chance of having a positive impact?

Joanna Frank   You shape it in an economic way. If you take health care costs. Health care has a massive cost to it. A third of the population will have diabetes in the next generation. This will bring down the economy faster than the environment, faster than anything else. It's an easy economic argument to make.

Rich Dallam   The country next to us, in terms of GDP, spent on health care has a difference of a trillion dollars. That trillion dollars is going to somebody for their economic benefit. So you are going to have people fighting back, unless you can reframe it so that they can make money from doing something that actually contributes. The line is that I'm going to come up with an oil for frying my food that doesn't kill me and that doesn't make me fat.

Karen Lee   This point that there is money to be made, and there are market forces that are actively shaping things potentially for the worse. That is why there is a role to play. The question of should we be designing to make things better is in some ways social engineering. The reality is that we are not acting in a vacuum where things are otherwise neutral. There are actually things actively being designed.

Whether economic or physical, there are economic forces that are actually leading people toward detrimental outcomes, both socially and healthwise, for various populations most vulnerable. The social engineering is occurring, so some of what we do is actually to counter some of that.

Gina Lovasi   Using the analogy to super-size is very interesting. You [Rich] were talking about houses being oversized, and I think in both cases we are shifting the norm of what is enough. It creates a moving target. I think the conversation around the soda size restrictions was, in a lot of ways, effective in shifting the public awareness about historical standards and, in a way, we could have the same thing with housing.

Leah Meisterlin   The soda discussion sparked a conversation and thus changed a cultural issue to a small extent. Whether or not the soda policy would have been effective is a different thing, but it did have a cultural effect to the extent to which design can be used to produce cultural changes, cultural awareness or perceptions that aren't necessarily reactionary. More than a behaviorist design approach, or in the interest of public health and public well-being, we need to come up with what big pharm is doing or what the soda industry is doing. If we can start to think about how to leapfrog over all of that and change the cultural expectations could be a powerful charge for designers.

> **Thomas De Monchaux**   That notion of getting designers out of that reactionary stance is so important. I am again reminded of this conversation I had with the head of the health care group about what the process and the conversation are like. He said that his designers are afraid of the doctors. The doctors are scary because the doctors are from the world of science. As architects we just swoon at science. Fetishization of data and parametrics. We are not immune to this in Morningside Heights. So there is that type of reactivity, and then there is this type of social reactivity. When you go to get your checkup, you don't want to spend a minute longer in that room than you have to because that's the room of death. You want to shorten that conversation with the doctor because the doctor is the angel of death. This is what that guy was saying.

Leah Meisterlin   You are only there when things are bad because of our system.

> **Thomas De Monchaux**   So you internalize this type of personal relationship to medicine as intimidating, as not questioning the assumption of whatever the client, in this case medical services, are giving you. You are doing what you are told. What this guy was saying is the design professions need to be much more assertive, and we need to drive the conversation in a different way and question—

Rich Dallam   What will it take for the design profession to do that? You have to think of yourself as leaders and not take missions, and you have to have brilliant communication skills: the ability to listen and reframe what you want to say in words that your audience is going to understand. As long as we see ourselves as technicians, we are just doing pretty things and will be completely marginalized. Someone gave the stats of how many people graduate with a master of architecture versus master of business administration per year. There are 189,000 MBAs to 7,000 MArchs nationally. You are outnumbered more than twenty to one. So if you can't talk or at least appreciate their economic language, you are going to be at such a disadvantage. All your great ideas will just get ignored. I think that is part of the framing issue. Our leadership, our communication and actually understanding your audience well enough to actually relate in terms that they understand. They are intimidated by aesthetics because they were never trained in it.

TYPICAL SECURITY PROTECTING ELEMENTARY SCHOOL, JOHANNESBURG

AERIAL VIEW OF URBAN PLANNING IN JOHANNESBURG

Thomas De Monchaux   The only thing I don't agree with, in terms of what you are saying, is about the default settings, especially when you are talking between wellness and design. We are stuck with some amazing discursive defaults of the city as a body, and generally the city as a sick body. The parks are always lungs; train stations are always hearts, or whatever. We've so internalized this metaphor that I don't know what quite to suggest we do about this. It's just the ultimate default setting. There must be ways to open it up and make us react to the body.

Mia Zinni [Student]   I have a comment bringing us back to what we saw in Johannesburg. One of the things that has come up today is this conflict between coming in as top-down designers or bottom-up by looking at the needs of groups that may be under a huge amount of stress. We had the opportunity to visit an office in Johannesburg where they did a studio project in a slum, and one of the outcomes from students meeting with residents was not designing very much. The community really wanted them to do very little. The students were frustrated with that, but the professors were saying it was okay because of the interaction and making some improvements. Later in the trip, we also heard about these moments where slums are completely wiped out by fire. This whole conversation has been more about health on a day-to-day basis, but what about those events where the built conditions create horrible opportunities for extreme incidents of devastating health? How do we as architects go in and have a conversation with the community about their day-to-day health, but also facilitate the realization that there might be a worse condition that can occur? How do we deal with those two levels of health—the day versus the extreme event?

Karen Lee   I think very frequently how participatory processes are structured, and the process by which they occur is actually really important. For example, you could have people at the table in a participatory process that have different levels of knowledge. So, in fact, we've begun at the Health Department over the last couple of years to do something called Community Active Design Workshops. They are charrette-type processes, but we don't merely bring the community together and then say, "Give us your ideas on what you want to see." We actually start with a presentation on what we know about active design and how it can shape various aspects of health as well as the benefits. We have a panel where community members, local business, etc., can actually talk about what they've done and the types of things they might have been involved with in a community active-design process to create change within their neighborhoods. Then the community, the folks who are there, will go to their tables and brainstorm ideas for a particular site that could use their ideas for improvements. Now the reason for actually having the panel and some of that background is so that everyone in the room is brought to a baseline level of knowledge about how the environment and built conditions are shaping things that might be important to the community, including their health.

179

Urban Health and Architecture

So when it comes time to actually brainstorm, everyone is at a base level of knowing what well-designed parks will potentially contribute to the community. So I think the discourse and the way the discourse is structured is actually really important. The types of issues you bring to the table as part of that discourse, whether they are day-to-day health and living conditions or larger key events that could occur because of the design of the community. Those are all things that could be brought to the table, but if they are on the table, then the discourse and the brainstorming with the community's input can include that. If they aren't on the table, then some people might think of it and others may very well not, just depending on who shows up at that conversation. So I think the structuring of that participatory discourse is quite important to what will actually occur in that discourse.

Allison Schwartz [student]   My question is about density in general. Different neighborhoods in South Africa, in Johannesburg in particular, have densities tied to planning under apartheid, as it was used as a method of control. This has resulted in a national housing shortage, as well as many low-density neighborhoods on the city's periphery. Additionally, like in parts of the U.S., there is an attachment to single-family housing as a shared cultural dream to someday have your own house with your own piece of land. I am working in an area that is incredibly dense with informal structures, and I've had trouble figuring out what is the right density to design for at the site. This is a complicated issue because, coming from New York, we have this mentality that density is good, but how do you measure a healthy density for Johannesburg? Similar to what was mentioned before with New York City and the trees, when have you reached the right level of access to parks and trees? What is a healthy level for people to be living with each other?

Karen Lee   I think that's actually a really great question because one of the things that I've been pushing for in the health world, for a while now, has been around the parameters of the built environment that shape health. Very frequently the way health studies are done are on a relative scale, so they might look at denser communities and less dense communities. They put them in quartiles and then they may compare the top quartile and the bottom quartile of communities to see if there is more walking and healthy behaviors in the top quartile as compared to the bottom quartile. Well, that's all well and great, and we've needed that generation of evidence to say higher density is associated with more walking, more activity, lower obesity, better health outcomes as relates to today's issues. I think in the next generation of evidence that we really need to start to define those thresholds, because, in practice, that's what you need—absolute values not relative values—if you are going to start to design a community or neighborhood that has a sufficient density but perhaps not a density so high that it becomes detrimental. So, I don't know, Gina, if you are able to comment on those thresholds because I really think in this next generation of evidence that we really need to start to find those thresholds so that we really can inform policies and practices. I would say, just to finish, that clearly we did have very severe densities in Lower Manhattan in the past, and they were too dense. There is a sense that if you have too much density and certainly overcrowding, there are potentially problems associated. At the same time, as our panelist who left said, the reality is that 88 percent of U.S. jurisdictions have way insufficient densities, and so I think there is a balance to be achieved. There is also density combined with other conditions. For example, Jonathan Rose Companies was mentioned as having done some good things. When Jonathan Rose spoke at Fit City a number of years ago, he said that what he strives for is density with green space. Green space for meditation and relaxation but also green space for physical activity. So, it's density, but it is also the combination with other built environment parameters, like green space, that achieves some sort of sufficient density without a density too high that leads to overcrowding and the spread of disease. Gina, can you comment on emerging research that starts to define these thresholds, because unfortunately a lot of the research has not defined these thresholds.

Gina Lovasi   So I think that there have been a number of thresholds proposed. Although, when we look, it seems like a linear relationship of housing density. I think distinguishing crowding from housing density is really important. How many people you have per room versus how many units you have. Also distinguishing what we want out of that image of the single-family home is partially about control and partially, in regards to other parts of the conversation, about security and having a private space. These are the fundamental things that we want out of a home, so figuring out ways to create that in small spaces is going to be really important.

Discussion

Urban Health and Architecture

Hillbrow

Hillbrow, a once prominent neighborhood of central Johannesburg, today is a low-income, primarily immigrant area. Residential towers are in decay and disrepair, yet nearby buildings are being renovated and painted in vibrant colors, signaling a recuperation. Walking through the neighborhood enabled students to see the buildings up close and at the ground level to better understand issues around entry, identity, and sense of place.

Soweto

The area of more than 25 townships founded under apartheid for non-whites has become known at Soweto, an abbreviation for South Western Townships. What has become a symbol of apartheid racial segregation, Soweto covers a wide area and its Townships are diverse, ranging middle class to informal settlements. The townships were built to address the shortage of housing for the black population in Johannesburg, estimated to be around 50,000 families in 1948. The layout of Soweto was primarily planned as single-family houses built by the government, planned at a peri-urban low density. Interspersed in the low-density neighborhoods are single-sex dormitory housing known as hostels that were built for transient workers.

Alexandra

Alexandra Township, familiarly known as Alex, is one of the densest areas in the city. Estimates vary drastically, but approximately 500,000 people live within an area of land roughly the size of Manhattan's Central Park. At 55,300 people per square mile, it is 10 times denser than the average 55,100-people-per-square-mile density of the metropolitan Johannesburg. Alex is composed of a combination of formal and informal dwellings with insufficient infrastructure for its population.

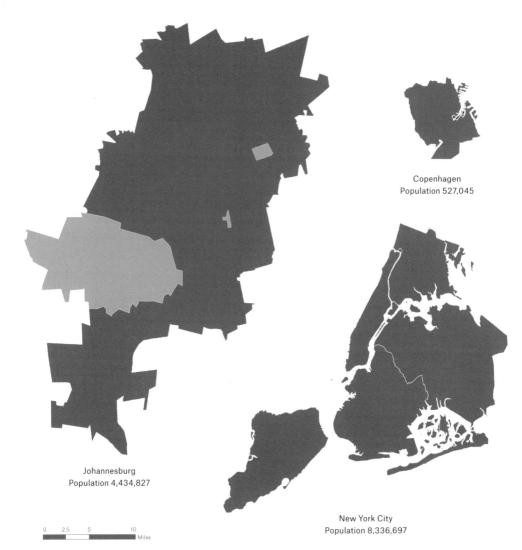

Copenhagen
Population 527,045

Johannesburg
Population 4,434,827

New York City
Population 8,336,697

```
0      2.5     5            10
                             Miles
```

Johannesburg: 2,696 ppl/km²
Hillbrow: 72,708 ppl/km²
Soweto: 6,357 ppl/km²
Alexandra: 25,979 ppl/km²

Copenhagen: 6,827 ppl/km²

New York City: 10,640 ppl/km²
Manhattan: 27,227 ppl/km²

DENSITY COMPARISON
SOURCE: JOHANNESBURG: STATISTICS SOUTH AFRICA, 2011 PRELIMINARY
CENSUS; COPENHAGEN: STATISTICS DENMARK, 2013; NEW YORK CITY: UNITED
STATES CENSUS BUREAU STATE AND COUNTY QUICKFACTS, 2012.

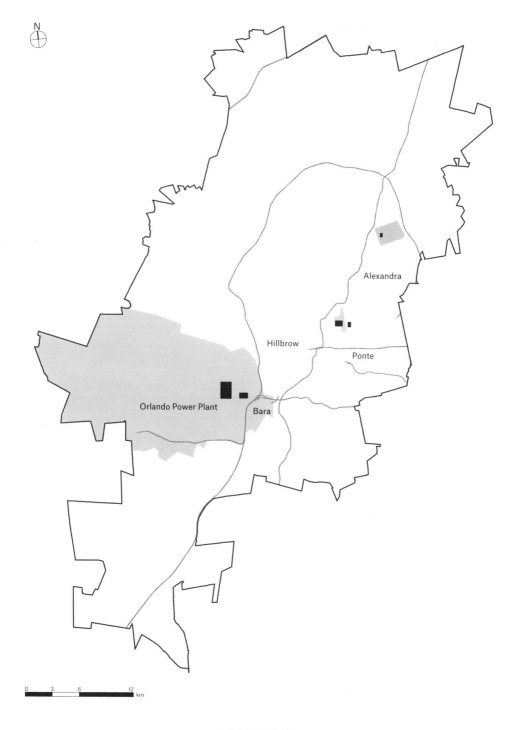

Orlando Power Plant

Hillbrow

Alexandra

Ponte

Bara

N

0   3   6   12
                    km

WALKING MAP KEY

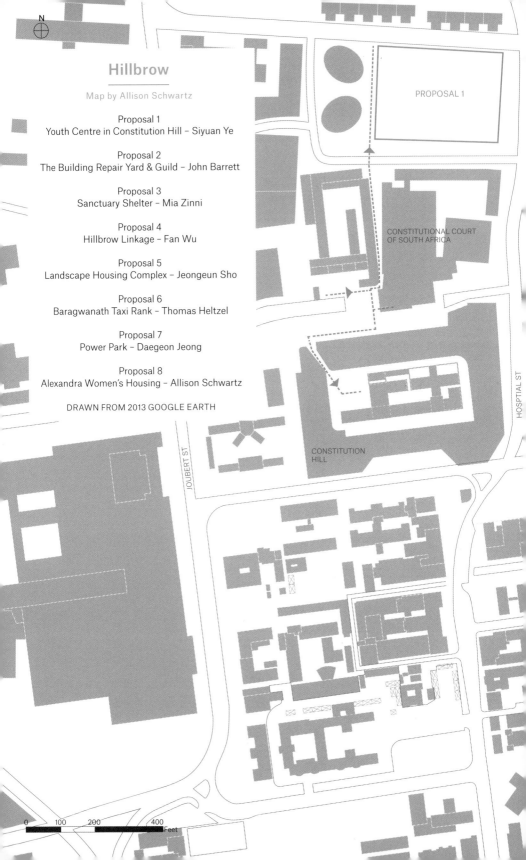

Hillbrow

Map by Allison Schwartz

Proposal 1
Youth Centre in Constitution Hill – Siyuan Ye

Proposal 2
The Building Repair Yard & Guild – John Barrett

Proposal 3
Sanctuary Shelter – Mia Zinni

Proposal 4
Hillbrow Linkage – Fan Wu

Proposal 5
Landscape Housing Complex – Jeongeun Sho

Proposal 6
Baragwanath Taxi Rank – Thomas Heltzel

Proposal 7
Power Park – Daegeon Jeong

Proposal 8
Alexandra Women's Housing – Allison Schwartz

DRAWN FROM 2013 GOOGLE EARTH

PROPOSAL 1

CONSTITUTIONAL COURT
OF SOUTH AFRICA

HOSPTIAL ST

JOUBERT ST

CONSTITUTION
HILL

0   100   200   400
Feet

VAN DER MERWE ST

PROPOSAL 3

DOCTOR & DENTIST
CLINICS

STREET
MARKET

PRETORIA ST

SURGERY
SHOP

SURGERY
SHOP

PROPOSAL 2

KOTZE ST

CLARENDON

ESSELEN ST

KAPTEIJN ST

KANI

KLEIN ST

EDITH CAVELL ST

TWIST ST

QUARTZ ST

LBROW HEALTH PRECINCT

THE PEDESTRIAN-ONLY COVERED MARKET ALONG QUARTZ STREET
RUNS THROUGH HILLBROW.

STREETS OF HILLBROW

ADVERTISEMENTS FOR INFORMAL HEALTH CARE
ARE PLASTERED ON BUILDINGS THROUGHOUT CITY.

WALK-IN CLINICS IN HILLBROW ADVERTISE THEIR HEALTH CARE OFFERINGS
IN THE WINDOW DISPLAYS.

Ponte

Map by Allison Schwartz

PONTE APARTMENT TOWER RISING FROM COMMERCIAL BASE

OCCUPIED ROOFTOPS

OPEN SITE ADJACENT TO THE TOWER

Bara

Map by Allison Schwartz

ENTRANCE TO BARAGWANATH HOSPITAL

MINI-BUS TAXIS CONNECT PASSENGERS LIVING IN THE LOW-DENSITY
HOUSING OF SOWETO WITH THE BARA INTERCHANGE,
A GATEWAY TO THE REST OF JOHANNESBURG.

TAXIS EXIT THE RANKING FACILITY AND HEAD TOWARD
CENTRAL JOHANNESBURG AND TO OTHER SOWETO
NEIGHBORHOODS.

THE INTERCHANGE PROVIDES THE ONLY PEDESTRIAN
CONNECTIONS TO CHRIS HANI BARAGWANATH HOSPITAL
VIA TWO BRIDGES OVER THE ROADWAY.

VENDORS LINE THE PASSAGEWAY LEADING TO THE HOSPITAL ENTRANCE.

VENDORS WITHIN THE MARKET HALL SELL FOOD, TRADITIONAL MEDICINE
AND OTHER SMALL ITEMS TO THE THOUSANDS OF PEOPLE THAT PASS
THROUGH THE INTERCHANGE DAILY.

Orlando Power Plant

Map by Allison Schwartz

MBAMBISA ST

MBAMBISA ST

PROPOSAL 2

ORLANDO POWER
STATION

CHRIS HANI RD

0   250   500   1000
                                   Feet

RECREATIONAL BUNGEE JUMPING BETWEEN
THE DECOMMISSIONED COOLING TOWERS IS NOW OFFERED.

VIEW OF ORLANDO POWER PLANT TOWERING OVER
THE MOSTLY SINGLE-LEVEL BUILDINGS OF SOWETO.

POWER LINES CONNECT SOWETO WITH
THE REST OF JOHANNESBURG.

Alexandra

Map by Allison Schwartz

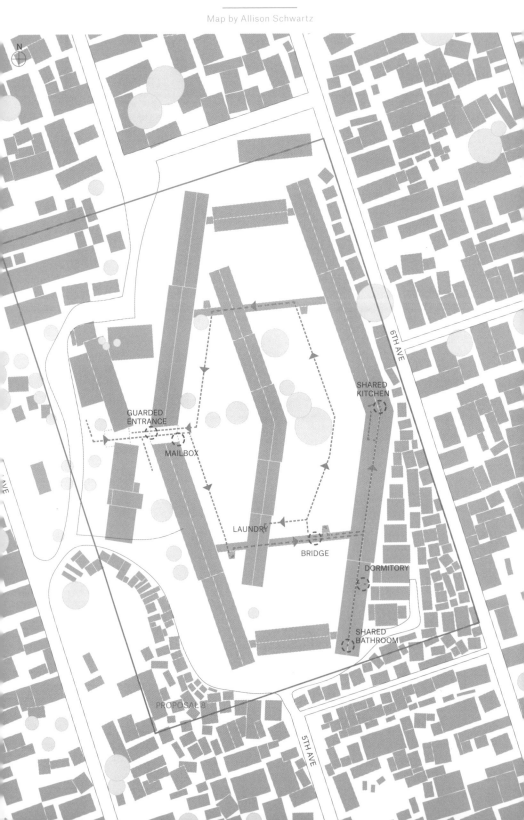

GATED AND MONITORED ENTRANCE TO WOMEN'S HOSTEL

THE ENORMITY OF THE HOSTEL STANDS IN
CONTRAST TO THE PRIMARILY INFORMALLY
CONSTRUCTED SURROUNDINGS.

THE UNDERUSED COURTYARD OF THE HOSTEL IS
ONE OF THE ONLY OPEN SPACES IN ALEXANDRA.

DORMITORIES WERE ORIGINALLY DESIGNED FOR FOUR WOMEN PER
ROOM. MANY WOMEN NOW HAVE THEIR CHILDREN LIVING WITH THEM.

COMMUNAL KITCHEN FACILITIES CONSIST OF SHARED GAS BURNERS,
SINKS, PREPARATION COUNTERS AND PICNIC BENCHES. EACH RESIDENT
RECEIVES A PERSONAL STORAGE LOCKER WITHIN THE KITCHEN.

THE LARGE COURTYARDS OF THE HOSTELS ARE
FILLED WITH DRYING LAUNDRY.

BRIDGED WALKWAYS CONNECT THE HOUSING BLOCKS
AND CONNECT TO THE VERTICAL CIRCULATION.

MAIL DISTRIBUTION FOR HOSTEL RESIDENTS
AT ENTRANCE OF BUILDING

BATHING FACILITIES ARE SHARED BY RESIDENTS OF EACH FLOOR.

Siyuan Ye

Playgrounds are virtually nonexistent in Johannesburg, and buildings for young people are also very rare in the city. Given this situation, the idea about how to create a specific place for young people to learn and share new experiences became essential to the project. According to the new urban form, playgrounds, study spaces, and relaxing areas will engage users to offer a healthy, enlightening environment for play, learning, and living. Additionally, public and private areas will benefit a new generation of

Johannesburg. The youth center is located in the northeast corner of Constitution Hill Precinct. The precinct is becoming one of the most popular attractions for both locals and tourists. Unlike other fenced public areas in Johannesburg, Constitution Hill Precinct is without any conspicuous obstruction, more open to the city but also safe. Therefore, the youth center built for this location would be a firm platform for students to review history and look forward to the future.

VIEW OF CENTER

205

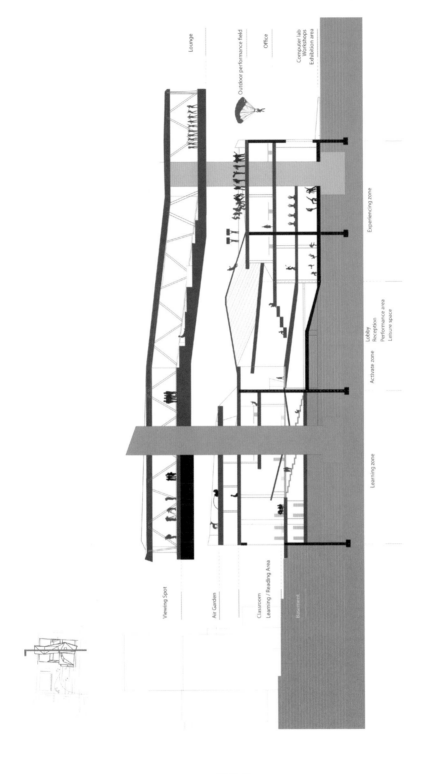

CENTER'S INTERIOR SPACE

Lounge

Outdoor performance field

Office

Computer lab
Workshops
Exhibition area

Experiencing zone

Lobby
Reception
Performance area
Leisure space

Activate zone

Learning zone

Viewing Spot

Air Garden

Classroom
Learning / Reading Area

Basement

The Building Repair Yard and Guild

John Barrett

Can a building be the agent of rejuvenation for a stressed urban environment? The Building Repair Guild and Yard proposes a new building typology that provides transitional housing, skill development, and the material repair of its neighborhood. Apprentices live beside mentors to learn new productive trades in a construction and materials facility called the Building Repair Yard. The Building Repair Yard provides a space of exchange for new and reclaimed building materials as well as facilities for the realization of larger-scale constructions that can alter and amend the existing built fabric of Johannesburg. The housing portion—suspended above the urban and working environments—combines short-term, incubator housing for transient populations with permanent housing to provide both vibrancy and safety to each group. The project facilitates a layered form of social life in which variously scaled "living room" spaces are shared (or not shared) with varying numbers of neighbors. Social networks are strengthened through a collection of private, semi-public, and public spaces where domestic life is lived largely in the open air.

209

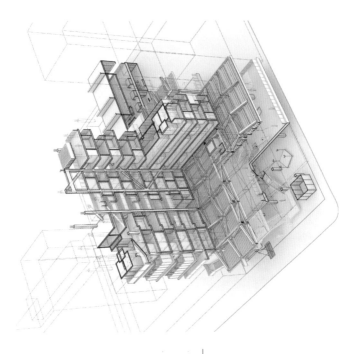

CUTAWAY SECTION–GUILD RESIDENCES AND BUILDING REPAIR YARD

SECTION–PUBLIC SPACE (YELLOW), BUILDING REPAIR YARD GUILD (ORANGE)

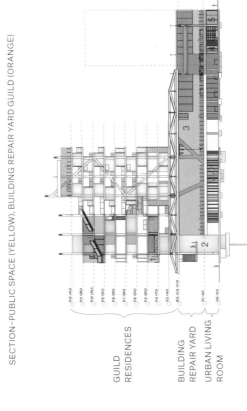

GUILD
RESIDENCES

BUILDING
REPAIR YARD

URBAN LIVING
ROOM

1. Medium Living Rooms
2. Public Platform
3. Common Shop (equip.)
4. Guild Canteen
5. BRY Store

OPEN PUBLIC STREET LEVEL

Proposals

Today, gender-based violence is one of the most prevalent and ignored violations of human rights. The United Nations estimates that acts of violence against women affect at least one out of every three women globally. The statistics in South Africa are grim. While it is estimated that only one in nine rapes are reported, the country still has the highest rate of reported rapes per capita in the world. Violence against women takes place principally at home and in other private spaces. Gender-based violence permeates rural and urban communities alike. Currently there exists a tension between secure "underground" women's shelters and women-empowerment organizations. Within the current urban conditions of Johannesburg, this project proposes a new typology for women. A secure sanctuary environment, which provides spaces for women to heal in solitude yet also creates outlets for communal growth fostering solidarity among women. The project operates on a two-tier programmatic strategy, providing immediate shelter and medical care to women along with more permanent housing and work opportunities for women partaking of extended stays. In order to secure, the architecture implements camouflage through a highly active market in front of the shelter. The market becomes a proletariat security system in which women own and operate stalls, simultaneously acting as security guards who monitor entry to the shelter's housing tower. The architecture mediates through gradients from safety to sanctuary and refuge to retreat, allowing women to feel secure without becoming prisoners of the space, creating introspective regions for individual healing.

ENTRY TO MAIN SANCTUARY SPACE

213

Proposals

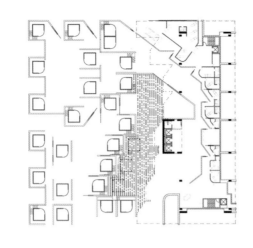

GROUND PLAN: SLIDING MARKET STALLS, BELOW-GRADE SANCTUARY SPACE AND EMERGENCY MEDICAL FACILITIES

PROGRAMMATIC EXPLODED AXON

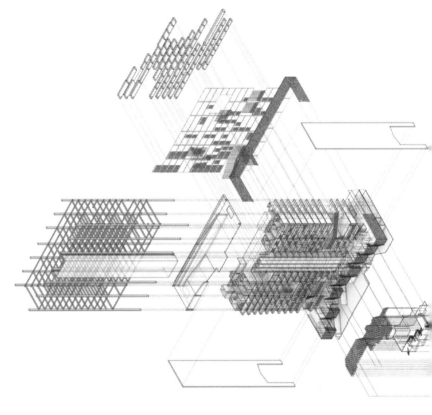

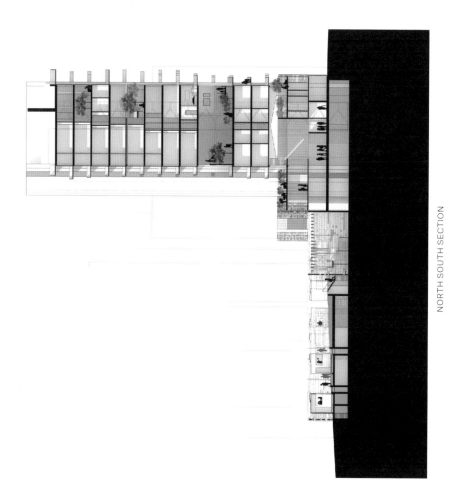

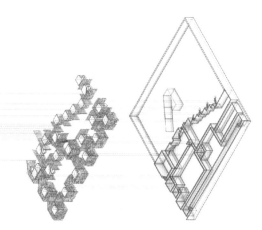

215

Proposals

Fan Wu

The project is a mixed-used building owned by Johannesburg University. At the same time, part of it opens to the Hillbrow community. On the community side, the orientation is toward a horizontal landscape, which creates a contrasting experience to the crowded urban space of Hillbrow, and may attract more users. As for the university side, it stands as a vertical tower. This could satisfy the university's need for more space. Flexible campus spaces are located within the tower. A communication platform connects the community side with the university side. Moreover, adding slopes surrounding the platform would serve to enhance the accessibility between two sides.

LANDSCAPE AND MIXED-USE BLOCK FOR HILLBROW LINKAGE

217

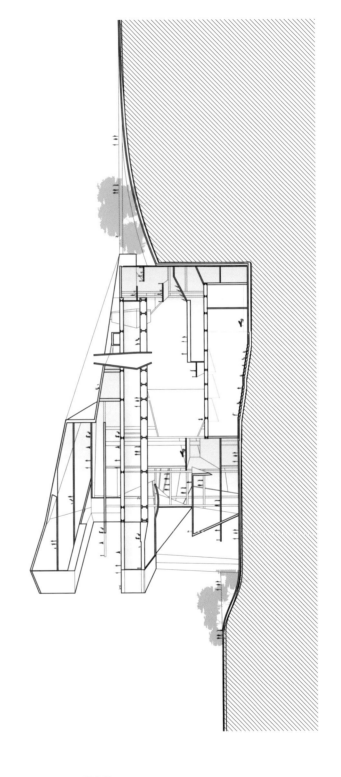

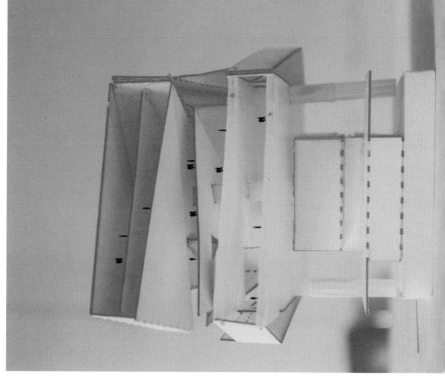

219

Proposals

Jeongeun Sho

The project's site is an existing residential area in Soweto. In order to create a healthy and sustainable environment for the area, the project proposes a housing redevelopment informed by current circumstances.

The basic scheme suggests upper-level landscapes that will make a courtyard market with canopy places below instead of the typical new high-rise residential buildings. By doing this, residents can create their own self-sufficient markets and enjoy a more diverse relationship with green spaces.

The design consists of four spatial components: plate, bridge, structure, and building. Specifically based on the architectural characteristics of their relationships, three main program combinations (farm+multi market, parasol+exhibition or education, landscape+commercial) are in the proposal. Each program combination enhances that district's local environment by creating fields and inner spaces that trigger specific activities.

The attractive landscapes not only become sightseeing areas to energize the regional society, but they also directly help each resident by generating money from the derived programs. The design seeks to alleviate unhealthy housing problems not only by remodeling each house to be more modern and healthy, but also by creating upper-layer landscapes and open spaces that will improve the informal housing residents' economic opportunities firsthand. Because one of the fundamental causes of inadequate housing in South Africa is the unstable economic situation, just eradicating detrimental housing will not solve the root of the problem. For example, much of the housing in Soweto combines formal and informal construction. Partially as a result of the government's efforts to eliminate informal housing, many, in this city with high population growth, cannot afford formal housing and build within backyards. To address this issue, the project gives residents new places in which they can activate their economic options themselves.

LANDSCAPE AND COMMERCIAL AERIAL VIEW

221

223

Baragwanath Taxi Rank

Thomas Heltzel

Located opposite the Chris Hani Baragwarath Hospital and Potchefstroom Road—the main arterial road into Soweto—is the Bara Taxi Rank. It is the largest in Johannesburg and acts as the gateway between Soweto and the rest of the metropolitan area. All Soweto taxis converge here. This project rethinks the role of the Bara Taxi Rank, understanding that the qualities and experiences of this space play a critical part in the daily lives of Soweto's citizens. More than 70 percent of Soweto's commuters pass through Bara daily, and the workings of the rank provide opportunities for urban experiences other than just transportation. The rank will provide the typical program—ranking, loading, and drop-off spaces—as well as "drive-thru" clinics, recreational opportunities, a market, an assembly hall for the South African National Taxi Council, training and servicing spaces, maintenance facilities, and a drivers' club. This range of programs will be entwined in a new, thick, composite structure. An efficient matrix of loading and unloading routes is expanded and weaved (in all dimensions) with passenger circulation, markets, and health and recreation programs. By using the ability of the taxis to accommodate sectional movement, the rank will simultaneously

provide an efficient, oriented means of transfer from taxi to taxi, as well as access to vital programs in a dense, interactive environment. Circulation will accommodate and orient movement to the rank, the arrival and exit of private vehicles, and the arrival of emergency vehicles. The new space will provide an entrance to the complex that is fitting to the importance of Baragwanath Hospital.

ENTWINED PROGRAMS AND CIRCULATION

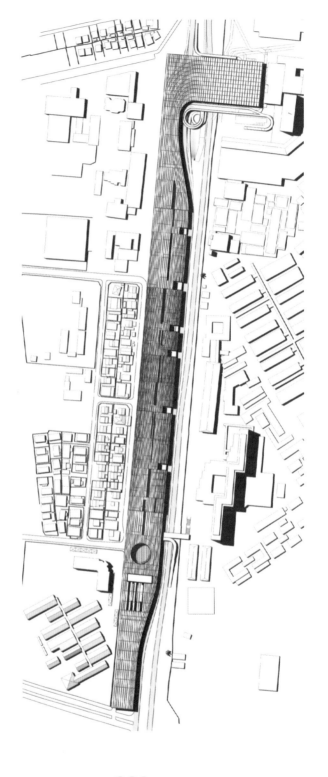

Heltzel

227

Proposals

The Orlando power plant is a post-industrial facility in Soweto. It served electricity to a large area of Johannesburg for fifty years. For this reason, the power plant became a symbol of Soweto, and the South African government has developed the decommissioned power plant as a tourist attraction. The project reorganizes this abandoned power plant to address current energy issues in the area. The lack of housing, insufficient supply of electricity, and poor hygienic conditions that exist in parts of Soweto have been ongoing problems for many years because of Soweto's history. The proposed program is a new sustainable power plant that uses the existing railroad and water resources on the site and links the power plant functions with the public, communal space. The new power plant includes a steam turbine, steam engine, and electricity storage, all facilitated by diverse energy resources, including the generation

of energy through biomass, photovoltaic, geothermal, and wind methods. Future energy-generating techniques can be incorporated into the power plant due to the built-in flexibility of the structure. Also, this model offers new programmatic relationships between the power plant and a variety of public spaces that include a spa, an energy research lab, a government office, and a theater to relieve the current lack of communal spaces in Soweto. The project draws on the new spatial experiences for the public in terms of program, scale, material, and structure to become a new city center for Soweto.

PERSPECTIVE OF THE NEW TURBINE ROOM

229

Proposals

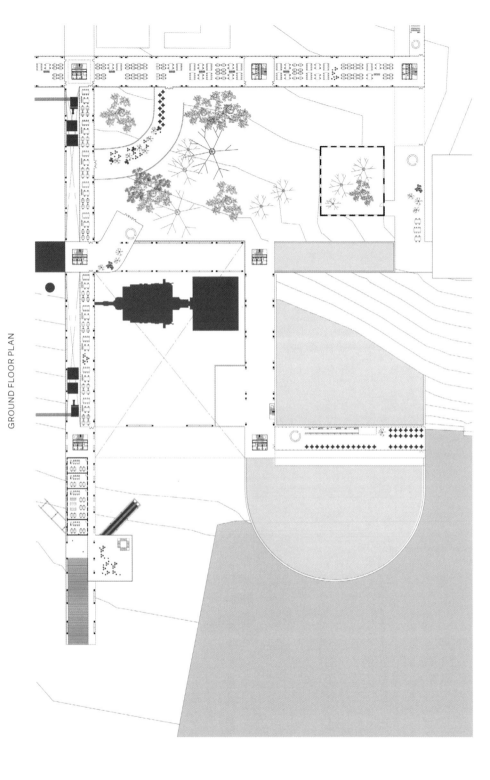

GROUND FLOOR PLAN

Jeong

SITE MODEL

231

Alexandra Women's Housing

Allison Schwartz

The Alexandra Women's Hostel in Johannesburg should be redeveloped to improve living conditions and offer increased opportunities to women in Alexandra. The redevelopment of the hostel will transform the apartheid architecture of control into an architecture of empowerment for the residents through the creation of occupant-determined spaces. This self-control of spaces occurs at multiple scales: the unit, the cluster, and the community. The manipulation of the multi-family typology, intermixed with access to services and educational opportunities, will provide an alternative model to the prevalent single-family house that is widely considered to be a stepping-stone to social mobility.

Phased construction reduces the number of displaced residents and allows the site to transform over time as funds become available and housing needs change. The existing hostel structure is broken to break up the enormous scale of the existing building and create variety within the housing. New bridges of shared programming between the existing structure will divide the open yard into smaller courtyard parks, creating housing clusters and encouraging more defined use of the open space.

A new sleeve of corridor and room extensions will wrap the existing building. This movement of corridors and stairs to the building's exterior will reduce the reliance on artificial lighting as well as increase visual access and activity around the courtyards, which promotes safer places through an eyes-on-the-street principle. The current location of the existing corridors within the central axes of the bars will be replaced with light wells to bring light and fresh air to the newly reconfigured units, as well as new wet cores for bathrooms and kitchens within the apartment units. The mix of female dormitories and women-owned apartments will bring new social and economic diversity to the building.

VIEW THROUGH COURTYARD TO NEW BRIDGING SHARED SPACES

233

VIEW THROUGH NEW EXTERIOR CORRIDOR

MODEL OF PHASED ADDITIONS TO EXISTING HOSTEL

SECTION THROUGH COURTYARD AND TWO BARS OF HOSTEL

235

Proposals

Acknowledgments

This book was made possible with the generosity and assistance of many people. First, I would like to thank the Graham Foundation for Advanced Studies in the Fine Arts for supporting my research project Sick City, on which this publication is based. In addition, I'd like to acknowledge the Graduate School of Architecture, Planning and Preservation's continued commitment to this research. As deans, both Mark Wigley and Amale Andraos have been incredibly thoughtful supporters of the project across its various phases, with acute sensitivity to the questions of urban health and urban scale that it raises. I am also grateful to NBBJ Architects, particularly Tim Johnson, Richard Dallam, Helen Dimoff, and Jay Siebenmorgen, without whom this publication, and the studio travel that preceded it, would not have happened.

From my travels in Johannesburg I want to thank Hannah Le Roux, who graciously agreed to join studios when we visited, and assisted in discussions before and after the trip; Terry Kurgan, Anthony Schneider, Mokena Makeka, Yael Horowitz, and Holly Fee from Wits Reproductive Health & HIV Institute and the Hillbrow Health Precinct project; and Kylie Dickson. I want to thank Mpho Matsipa, who made significant introductions that enabled us to visit parts of Johannesburg we would not otherwise have been able to. Mabel Wilson, Laura Kurgan, Mario Gooden, and Ada Tolla for serving as sounding boards and continuing the conversations around health as it particularly relates to housing. I also want to mention all of the panelists who visited the studio: Vishaan Chakrabarti, Marc Norman, Joanna Frank, Leah Meisterlin. The studio served as a test session for the later Conversations around Health, Architecture, and Cities that was co-sponsored by GSAPP and the Mailman School of Public Health. I would also like to thank Dean Sandro Galea for joining the studio and the conversation. Work done by Dr. Gina Lovasi, Dr. Andrew Rundle, and Dr. Karen Lee provided guidance and inspiration in finalizing this book. I want to thank those who contributed to the book, and especially Lindsay Bremner, not only for her work but for her continued interest in the project. I want to thank Guy Tillim for generously contributing his incredible photographs to the book and for the cover. I also want to sincerely thank Susan Szenasy for publishing an early text and setting the stage for the students' work to be published in *Metropolis*. In the school's Office of Publications, Director James Graham and editors Jordan Carver and Caitlin Blanchfield provided outstanding editorial guidance. Luke Bulman's graphic design work uplifted the project at every step. I would also like to thank Allison Schwartz, a member of the studio who worked tirelessly and dedicated her time just after graduation to thoughtfully manage this project and its ever-increasing parts. Their dedication helped to bring this collection of work into print. My students were also an invaluable source of insight both in the classroom and during our research in Johannesburg. The creativity of their work is a testament to the rich work to be done at the intersection of architecture and public health.

Image Credits

p. 130 ("Global Regions of Thermic Sultriness Values"): Courtesy of Augustus C. Long Health Sciences Library.

p. 8-9: © Guy Tillim

"Shandukani"
p. 41: Courtesy of GVK-Siya Zama Building Construction (Gauteng) (pty) Ltd.

"Jo'burg"
All images © Guy Tillim

"Geological Health"
p. 68: Courtesy of William Cullen Library, University of Johannesburg

"Inspired Hope from an Icon of Decay"
p. 88, 90-94: © 2013 Google CDNGI Digital Globe

"Taxi Rank No. 2"
p. 100-101: © Dave Southwood
p. 104, 106: © Iwan Baan

"Urban Health Maps"
p. 130, 132: Courtesy of US Navy Bureau of Medicine and Surgery (BIMED) archives.

"Carlton Centre"
p. 161: © Ezra Stoller/Esto

Stress and Wellness in Johannesburg

GSAPP Books
An imprint of The Graduate School of Architecture, Planning and Preservation
Columbia University
407 Avery Hall
1172 Amsterdam Avenue
New York, NY   10027
Visit our website at www.arch.columbia.edu/publications

Library of Congress Cataloging-in-Publication Data
Questions concerning health : stress and wellness in Johannesburg / [edited by] Hilary Sample.
pages cm
Includes index.
ISBN 978-1-883584-92-4
1. City planning—Health aspects—South Africa—Johannesburg.
2. Architecture—Health aspects—South Africa—Johannesburg.
3. Public health—South Africa—Johannesburg.
4. Urban health—South Africa—Johannesburg.
5. Community health services—South Africa—Johannesburg.
I. Sample, Hilary, editor of compilation.
RA566.7.Q47 2015
362.1096822'1—dc23
2015002269

This book has been produced through the Office of the Dean, Amale Andraos,
with production coordination by James Graham and Caitlin Blanchfield,
Office of Publications.

This book was made possible through the generous support of NBBJ Architects.

Graphic Design: Thumb/Luke Bulman with Celine Gordon and Camille Sacha Salvador
Copy Editor: Ellen Tarlin
Printer: Regal Printing Limited